Understanding
American History

The Constitution and the Founding of a New Nation

Hal Marcovitz

Bruno Leone
Series Consultant

ReferencePoint Press®

San Diego, CA

© 2014 ReferencePoint Press, Inc.
Printed in the United States

For more information, contact:
ReferencePoint Press, Inc.
PO Box 27779
San Diego, CA 92198
www. ReferencePointPress.com

LIBRARY OF CONGRESS CATALOGING-IN-PUBLICATION DATA

Marcovitz, Hal.
  The constitution and the founding of a new nation / by Hal Marcovitz.
    pages cm. -- (Understanding American history)
  Includes bibliographical references and index.
  ISBN-13: 978-1-60152-594-9 (hardback)
  ISBN-10: 1-60152-594-X (hardback)
  1. Constitutional history--United States--18th century--Juvenile literature. 2. United States--Politics and government--1783–1789--Juvenile literature. I. Title.
  KF4541.M298 2014
  342.7302'9--dc23
                                                                          2013006478

Contents

Foreword   4

Important Events in the History of the Constitution
and the Founding of a New Nation   6

Introduction   8
  What Are the Defining Characteristics
  of the US Constitution?

Chapter One   13
  What Conditions Led to the Need for the
  Constitution and the Founding of a New Nation?

Chapter Two   26
  Crises in the New Nation

Chapter Three   39
  A Summer in Philadelphia

Chapter Four   52
  The Road to Ratification

Chapter Five   66
  What Is the Legacy of the Constitution and
  Its Role in the Founding of a New Nation?

Source Notes   81

Important People in the History of the Constitution
  and the Founding of a New Nation   85

For Further Research   88

Index   91

Picture Credits   96

About the Author   96

Foreword

America's Puritan ancestors—convinced that their adopted country was blessed by God and would eventually rise to worldwide prominence—proclaimed their new homeland the shining "city upon a hill." The nation that developed since those first hopeful words were uttered has clearly achieved prominence on the world stage and it has had many shining moments but its history is not without flaws. The history of the United States is a virtual patchwork of achievements and blemishes. For example, America was originally founded as a New World haven from the tyranny and persecution prevalent in many parts of the Old World. Yet the colonial and federal governments in America took little or no action against the use of slave labor by the southern states until the 1860s, when a civil war was fought to eliminate slavery and preserve the federal union.

In the decades before and after the Civil War, the United States underwent a period of massive territorial expansion; through a combination of purchase, annexation, and war, its east–west borders stretched from the Atlantic to the Pacific Oceans. During this time, the Industrial Revolution that began in eighteenth-century Europe found its way to America, where it was responsible for considerable growth of the national economy. The United States was now proudly able to take its place in the Western Hemisphere's community of nations as a worthy economic and technological partner. Yet America also chose to join the major western European powers in a race to acquire colonial empires in Africa, Asia, and the islands of the Caribbean and South Pacific. In this scramble for empire, foreign territories were often peacefully annexed but military force was readily used when needed, as in the Philippines during the Spanish-American War of 1898.

Toward the end of the nineteenth century and concurrent with America's ambitions to acquire colonies, its vast frontier and expanding industrial base provided both land and jobs for a new and ever-growing wave of immigrants from southern and eastern Europe. Although America had always encouraged immigration, these newcomers—Italians, Greeks, and eastern European Jews, among others—were seen as different from the vast majority of earlier immigrants, most of whom were from northern and western Europe. The presence of these newcomers was treated as a matter of growing concern, which in time evolved into intense opposition. Congress boldly and with calculated prejudice set out to create a barrier to curtail the influx of unwanted nationalities and ethnic groups to America's shores. The outcome was the National Origins Act, passed in 1924. That law severely reduced immigration to the United States from southern and eastern Europe. Ironically, while this was happening, the Statue of Liberty stood in New York Harbor as a visible and symbolic beacon lighting the way for people of *all* nationalities and ethnicities seeking sanctuary in America.

Unquestionably, the history of the United States has not always mirrored that radiant beacon touted by the early settlers. As often happens, reality and dreams tend to move in divergent directions. However, the story of America also reveals a people who have frequently extended a helping hand to a weary world and who have displayed a ready willingness—supported by a flexible federal constitution—to take deliberate and effective steps to correct injustices, past and present. America's private and public philanthropy directed toward other countries during times of natural disasters (such as the contributions of financial and human resources to assist Haiti following the January 2010 earthquake) and the legal right to adopt amendments to the US Constitution (including the Thirteenth Amendment freeing the slaves and the Nineteenth Amendment granting women the right to vote) are examples of the nation's generosity and willingness to acknowledge and reverse wrongs.

With objectivity and candor, the titles selected for the Understanding American History series portray the many sides of America, depicting both its shining moments and its darker hours. The series strives to help readers achieve a wider understanding and appreciation of the American experience and to encourage further investigation into America's evolving character and founding principles.

1215
Reacting to heavy taxes imposed by King John, English barons raise their own army and force the king to affix the royal seal to the Magna Carta, which limits the rule of the British monarch and establishes rights for subjects.

1754
The French and Indian War erupts in western Pennsylvania; American colonists are forced to fight on the side of the British and help pay for the war, which causes friction in the colonies and hostility toward the king and Parliament.

1610
A new governor, Thomas West, arrives at the Jamestown colony in Virginia and, to restore order in the colony, enacts the Laws Divine, Moral and Martial.

1735
John Peter Zenger goes on trial in New York for libeling the royal governor. His acquittal establishes the principle of freedom of the press in America.

1200	1600	1650	1700	1750

1620
Colonists aboard the *Mayflower* arrive at Plymouth Bay in Massachusetts and before leaving the ship write the Mayflower Compact as a framework of governance for their colony.

1765
Parliament passes the Stamp Act, which assesses widespread taxes on the American colonies. Colonial leaders convene the Stamp Act Congress, in which the levy is denounced as taxation without representation.

1773
Parliament passes the Tea Act, which forces the American colonies to accept tea exported from England. The act leads to the protest known as the Boston Tea Party, followed by harsh measures enacted by Parliament to ensure British law is followed in the colonies.

1641
The Massachusetts Body of Liberties, one of the first sets of laws to govern an American colony, is adopted by the Massachusetts Assembly.

1788
On June 21 the New Hampshire Assembly ratifies the Constitution, providing the minimum nine-state approval necessary for the document to become the nation's supreme law.

1787
The Constitutional Convention begins in Philadelphia; for more than four months delegates debate the powers of the federal government. On September 17 a majority of delegates sign the new US Constitution, sending it to the states for ratification.

1783
The Treaty of Paris ratifies the independence of the thirteen North American states, officially ending the state of war.

1785
Heavily burdened by debts incurred during the War of Independence, the Continental Congress defaults on its obligation to repay $2 million borrowed from the French government.

1775
The first shots in the War of Independence are fired at Lexington and Concord in Massachusetts.

1780   1782   1784   1786   1788

1781
British general Lord Charles Cornwallis surrenders to George Washington following the Battle of Yorktown in Virginia, essentially ending the War of Independence.

1789
Congress debates and sends the Bill of Rights—the first ten amendments to the Constitution—to the states for ratification.

1791
The Bill of Rights becomes law.

1776
On July 4 the Declaration of Independence is signed in Philadelphia.

1786
On August 29 Shays's Rebellion breaks out when angry farmers, led by Daniel Shays, shut down the courthouse in Northampton, Massachusetts, to prevent a judge from ordering the seizures of land owned by local farmers.

What Are the Defining Characteristics of the US Constitution?

When the US Constitution was written during the summer of 1787, medical science was in its infancy. Few hospitals or medical schools existed in American cities. Doctors had limited tools available for treating disease, mending broken bones, or diminishing pain. In fact, the average life expectancy during the era was less than forty years. Whatever medical care was available was relatively inexpensive, and in rural areas doctors were often paid with livestock, eggs, or grain rather than cash.

And so when the delegates to the Constitutional Convention provided Congress with the power to levy taxes, it is unlikely they envisioned that authority applied to making health care widely available. In fact, their main concern in granting Congress the power to levy taxes was to pay off debts that remained from the War of Independence.

But in 2012 the US Supreme Court declared the controversial Patient Protection and Affordable Care Act constitutional, finding that the law's provision giving Congress the power to assess fees on people who do not buy health insurance falls under the constitutional authority to levy taxes granted to lawmakers more than two centuries ago. Wrote Chief Justice John Roberts, "It is reasonable to construe what Congress has done as increasing taxes on those who have a certain amount of income, but choose to go without health insurance. Such legislation is within Congress's power to tax."[1]

The Supreme Court's decision illustrates how the Constitution has proved to be a resilient document, enabling judges to find its terms applicable to facets of American society that did not exist in the eighteenth century. Says University of Chicago Law School professor David A. Strauss:

> The written US Constitution, the document under glass in the National Archives, was adopted more than 220 years ago. . . . Meanwhile, the world has changed in incalculable ways. The United States has grown in territory, and its population has multiplied several times. Technology has changed, the international situation has changed, the economy has changed—all in ways that no one could have foreseen when the Constitution was drafted.[2]

Challenging the Law

In the three years preceding the Supreme Court's decision, no issue seemed to divide the American people as much as the Affordable Care Act. The measure seeks to ensure virtually all Americans access to medical services, including physician visits, medications, and hospital stays. Over the years, many people found that due to the spiraling cost of medical care, these services, as well as the health insurance that would help make them available, were often unaffordable. By 2009 it was estimated that some 30 million Americans did not have the money to see a doctor.

As he campaigned for the presidency in 2008, then–Illinois senator Barack Obama pledged to help make medical care affordable. Soon after Obama was inaugurated as president in 2009, his allies in Congress drafted bills that took numerous steps toward making health insurance and medical care within reach for most Americans. Congress debated the bills for months, and finally, after close votes in both the House and Senate, the Affordable Care Act was adopted and signed into law by the president.

The US Constitution became the nation's supreme law in 1788, just five years after the official end of the War of Independence. The Constitution, which played a seminal role in the founding of the new nation, continues to guide and shape modern life in the United States.

The law was soon challenged in the courts by those who believed the government had overstepped its authority. Their main argument focused on the component of the act that assesses fees on people who refuse to buy health insurance. Opponents, including the governors and attorneys general of twenty-six states, contended the government could not force somebody to buy something that he or she did not want to own—not even insurance that would help guarantee that person access to a doctor or hospital. "Congress does not have the power to compel Kansans to participate in healthcare finance schemes against their will,"[3] insisted Kansas governor Sam Brownback, who, as a member of the Senate in 2009, voted against the Affordable Care Act.

The challenges to the Affordable Care Act made their way through the American judicial system until finally the Supreme Court agreed to hear arguments and rule on the law. In a 5–4 vote, with Roberts breaking the tie, the nation's highest court threw out the challenges to the Affordable Care Act and permitted it to stand. "The federal government does not have the power to order people to buy health insurance," wrote Roberts. "The federal government does have the power to impose a tax on those without health insurance."[4]

Impact Felt by All Americans

Although the Constitution can be applied to circumstances that were unknown in the eighteenth century—such as a crisis in American health care—in many respects, the political system established by the Constitution remains unchanged in the more than 220 years in which the document has served as the law of the land. The process under which laws are written, adopted, signed, and interpreted is identical to the process that existed in the final years of the eighteenth century. The Affordable Care Act, for example, was written and adopted by a legislative body created under article 1 of the Constitution. In signing and implementing the law, the president carried out duties spelled out in article 2. The Supreme Court, which upheld the law, was established in article 3, which grants the court the power to interpret the Constitution. And since the law was written, signed, and upheld in accordance with the Constitution, its impact will be felt by all Americans.

Of course, the Constitution does much more than establish a federal bureaucracy and the rules under which the president and members of Congress do their jobs. The Constitution has defined basic American rights—such as the rights to free speech, assembly, fair trials, and equal treatment under law. Over the years, the Constitution has been amended to address specific ills in American society—such as granting freedom to slaves, guaranteeing women the right to vote, removing taxes assessed on people at the polls, and establishing the process under which the vice president or congressional leaders ascend to the presidency in the event the president cannot finish his or her term. In fact, the way in which the Constitution can be amended was also written into the Constitution under the terms of article 5.

These provisions as well as others devised by the framers of the Constitution have managed to endure for more than two centuries. Says University of Pennsylvania historian Richard Beeman:

> The American experiment in liberty and constitutional governance has had its rocky moments, but our Constitution has not only proven to be the world's most durable written frame of government, but it is also, I believe, its most just and equitable. The men who drafted it knew that they had not created a "perfect" constitution, but they were nevertheless committed to continuing the quest for a "more perfect union."[5]

Chapter 1

What Conditions Led to the Need for the Constitution and the Founding of a New Nation?

By the 1700s thirteen English colonies had been established in America—each with a representative government, and each with a specific set of laws to govern its subjects. Among these documents were the Connecticut Resolves, the Massachusetts Body of Liberties, and the Maryland Act for the Liberties of the People. These laws were largely similar, granting colonists free assembly, freedom of speech, fair trials, and other basic rights. For example, the Massachusetts Body of Liberties, adopted in 1641, included ninety-eight statutes under which colonists were to be governed. The Body of Liberties made it clear that all people were to be treated equally under the law. "Every person within this Jurisdiction, whether Inhabitant or foreigner, shall enjoy the same justice and law that is general . . . which we constitute and execute one toward another without partiality or delay,"[6] reads the second statute.

Other statutes reflect the needs as well as fears of the era. The eighteenth statute established the circumstances under which colonists accused

The Code of Hammurabi

The phrase "an eye for an eye," suggesting that punishments should reflect the severity of the crimes, is commonly heard today. The phrase is drawn from the translation of tablets inscribed with laws written by King Hammurabi, who ruled the city-state of Babylon—a region that was located in what is now Iraq—from 1792 BC to 1750 BC.

The Code of Hammurabi is believed to be the first body of laws rendered into written form. Hammurabi was a monarch who ruled with absolute authority, but his authorship of a code of laws indicates he desired his subjects to know the rule of law was not arbitrary and would be applied equally. Says Marc Van De Mieroop, professor of ancient history at Columbia University, "His close to 300 laws prescribe what to do in cases of theft, murder, professional negligence, and many other areas in the daily lives of the people whom he ruled. They are often regarded as the earliest expression of ideas of justice, which are still with us today."

The laws established penalties for crimes as well as methods for solving disputes involving trade. For example, a tavern owner found to be cheating a customer risked a sentence of being tossed into the Euphrates River. And a subject who returned a runaway slave to the owner could expect a reward of two pieces of silver from the owner. The death penalty was common—it could be imposed for infractions such as robbery as well as falsely accusing others of committing crimes.

Marc Van De Mieroop, *King Hammurabi of Babylon: A Biography.* Malden, MA: Blackwell, 2005, p. vii.

of crimes could post bail, while the forty-sixth ensured punishments were fair and imposed without cruelty. The ninety-fourth statute mandated the death penalty for an offense that was of much concern: "If any man or woman be a witch (that is, hath or consulteth with a familiar spirit), they shall be put to death."[7]

Although the American colonies enjoyed a large measure of autonomy, they nonetheless lived under British rule. From London, the king and Parliament sent royal governors to oversee the colonies, but these administrators were largely satisfied with letting the colonists govern themselves. Trade between the mother country and the colonies was brisk, as many crops grown on American farms and goods produced in colonial mills were shipped to Great Britain. But in 1754 a dispute in western Pennsylvania between French and English traders ignited the French and Indian War. The American colonists were obligated to fight on the side of the British. Colonial assemblies were forced to provide money as well as militiamen to the war effort—duties the assemblies generally resented. At the conclusion of the seven-year-long war, which Great Britain won, tensions between the colonists and the English government were high.

Taxing Molasses

Relations between the American colonies and the British remained tense for nearly two decades, as Parliament and the king continued to exert control over the colonists. For example, regiments of British soldiers remained in America after the war, and colonists often found themselves forced to provide rooms in their private homes to the soldiers—a practice known as "quartering" troops. In later years the authors of the US Constitution would include a provision specifically prohibiting the military from housing troops in the homes of American citizens.

It was the British government's taxation policies, however, that angered Americans above all else. To replenish the nation's treasury following the French and Indian War, Parliament resolved to raise revenue by taxing the colonies. In 1764 it passed the Sugar Act, levying a tax on sugar exported from the colonies. The tax was imposed on exporters of molasses, but farmers were quick to see its implications: To afford the tax, merchants would have to pay the sugarcane growers less for their crops.

Samuel Adams, a member of the colonial assembly in Massachusetts, published a pamphlet warning his state's farmers that if Parliament could levy a tax that would drive sugarcane prices down, the British would not hesitate to impose other taxes that could affect everyone's crop prices. "For if our trade be taxed, why not our lands?" Adams's pamphlet asked. "Why not the produce of our lands and, in short, everything we possess or make use of?"[8]

The Stamp Act Congress

A year later it appeared as though Adams's prediction was coming true. In 1765 Parliament passed the Stamp Act, which required colonists to pay taxes on the purchase and use of a variety of items, from newspapers and playing cards to legal documents.

Colonial leaders reacted harshly to the Stamp Act. In 1765 nine colonies sent representatives to what was known as the Stamp Act Congress, in which the delegates declared the stamp tax unfair because it was adopted by a parliament sitting some 3,500 miles (5,633 km) away from the people affected by it, and because the colonists had no voice in the decision to levy the tax. This was the origin of the concept "no taxation without representation," which became a guiding principle in American government in the years ahead and was later given the weight of law in the Constitution. The phrase is believed to have been coined by Boston politician and lawyer James Otis. During a 1764 meeting of the Boston town council, Otis shouted, "Taxation without representation is tyranny!"[9]

Delegates to the Stamp Act Congress also addressed concerns that had little to do with the taxes levied on the colonies. One resolution adopted by the Stamp Act Congress declared trial by jury a fundamental right of all colonists. In adopting the resolution, the delegates put words to their long-held belief that British judges sitting in colonial courts tended to rule against colonists, regardless of the evidence.

As for the tax imposed by the Stamp Act, the delegates called for a boycott of the levy. In colonial cities violence often erupted between colonists and the royal tax collectors as colonists refused to pay the tax. In England, Parliament responded by repealing the Stamp Act.

War of Independence

Nevertheless, Parliament continued to impose new taxes and laws on the colonists. In 1767 it adopted the Townshend Acts. Named after Charles Townshend, the chancellor of the exchequer (the chief financial officer of the British government), the Townshend Acts established the principle that Parliament held the right to tax the American colonies. A companion law, the Declaratory Act, stated, "[Parliament] hath, and of right ought to have, full power and authority to make laws and statutes of sufficient force and validity to bind the colonies and people of America . . . in all cases whatsoever."[10]

It was the Tea Act of 1773, though, that lit the first fuse of rebellion in the colonies. The Tea Act forced the colonists to accept cheap tea exported from London, undercutting the prices of tea grown in America. The Tea Act led to the infamous Boston Tea Party, in which colonists boarded ships anchored in Boston Harbor and dumped imported tea overboard.

This act of protest led Parliament to adopt measures to curtail the powers of the colonial assemblies, give wider powers to the royal governors, and dispatch more troops to America to impose order. These measures, known in the colonies as the Intolerable Acts, led in 1774 to the convening of the First Continental Congress in Philadelphia, at which delegates from twelve of the thirteen colonies resolved to boycott all trade with England. The British regarded this as an act of war, and in April 1775 the first shots in the War of Independence were fired at Lexington and Concord in Massachusetts. A year later the Continental Congress convened again in Philadelphia, and the Declaration of Independence, authored by Thomas Jefferson, was debated and adopted.

Boston citizens, many of whom are dressed as Native Americans, protest the Tea Act by dumping British tea into Boston Harbor in 1773. In the wake of this protest, known as the Boston Tea Party, Parliament adopted measures curtailing colonial powers.

Over the course of the six-year-long war, the thirteen colonies maintained separate assemblies, but the Continental Congress remained intact to mediate disputes among the loosely allied colonial governments and coordinate the war effort, mostly by raising and maintaining the Continental army, led by General George Washington. When the war ended in 1781 with the surrender of British general Lord Charles Cornwallis at Yorktown, Virginia, many of the new nation's leaders realized they could not return to the old system of individual assemblies and separate sets of laws for what were now thirteen independent states.

The Roman Republic
As they looked to the future, many of the new nation's political leaders knew the current system of thirteen independent states and gov-

ernments was unworkable. They were well aware of the need to establish a common system of laws for governing their new country. These leaders were educated men and therefore knowledgeable about historical attempts—and failures—to establish democratic systems of government with laws applied equally to all citizens. James Madison, for example, was fluent in Latin, the language of the ancient Romans. He had read the essays and diaries of the ancient Romans and was an admirer of Cicero, Tacitus, and Seneca—Romans who helped establish one of civilization's first republics.

Indeed, the idea that nations should be governed under a system of laws written and approved by their citizens did not originate in Philadelphia in the summer of 1787. Rather, the notion that citizens should be governed by a constitution dates back to 450 BC, when the Roman senate adopted a code of laws known as the Twelve Tables.

The Roman senate had been established by Romulus, the first ruler of Rome, who founded the city in the eighth century BC. To help him rule, Romulus appointed a one-hundred-member advisory council composed of the leaders of Rome's most powerful families. This council was known as the senate.

The senate's authority was limited, and in fact over the next three hundred years the real power in Rome was wielded by a series of monarchs. However, that changed in 509 BC when a despotic ruler, Tarquinius Superbus, was ousted in a popular rebellion. Afterward, the senate declared Rome would never again be ruled by a monarch and that Rome was now a *res publica*, the Latin term for "republic"—a community in which the power rests in the hands of the citizens who are governed by leaders they select, usually through popular votes. Ordinary citizens, or plebeians, were granted the rights of free speech and assembly along with other liberties. In 494 BC the senate widened Rome's republican form of government by creating assemblies of plebeians, giving them as well as the upper classes a voice in the government. Nevertheless, the Roman senate was still composed of wealthy aristocrats who often abused their positions, interpreting Roman law for their own benefit.

Laws Inscribed in Stone

In 450 BC plebeian leaders demanded that Roman law be applied equally to all. And to ensure this, they insisted the laws of the republic be put in writing. As such, these laws would be available for anyone to read and, therefore, could not be changed arbitrarily by those in power. Fearing a popular uprising, the senate agreed and ordered the creation of the Twelve Tables. These were not only rendered in written form, but to ensure they would be followed to the letter, they were inscribed in stone.

Some of the laws established in the Twelve Tables read as though they could be a part of a modern democratic constitution: They set down a procedure for fair trials and provided rules protecting citizens from harm inflicted by other citizens. Penalties for violating the Twelve Tables could be harsh—failure to pay off a debt, for example, could result in enslavement or even execution. Nevertheless, the Roman republic was now governed under a written set of laws that were approved by ordinary citizens and applied equally to everyone.

The Roman republic and its rule of law lasted for four centuries. In 27 BC a long civil war ended when the Roman aristocrat Octavius seized power and was granted unlimited authority by the Roman senate. Taking the name Augustus, he ruled as the first in a long line of emperors who reigned over Rome for the next five hundred years. In AD 476 the rule of the Roman emperors finally came to an end after decades of military defeats and the erosion of the empire. Rome, as well as the rest of Europe, entered the medieval era, during which people were ruled by feudal barons. Under the feudal system, the rights of ordinary people, the peasants, depended largely on the benevolence of the wealthy rulers who owned the land on which they lived. These aristocrats governed the peasantry with absolute authority.

The Magna Carta

Throughout Europe, the powerful monarchs who eventually emerged from this feudal system established national borders. Warfare among countries was common; one such conflict was a twelve-

Slow Evolution of Parliament

It was not until the late nineteenth century that the composition of the House of Commons in Parliament reflected most social classes that compose the British people. Before that, the upper classes maintained a firm hold on Parliament by denying the right to vote to most of the population.

The first move toward equality occurred in 1832, when Parliament passed the Reform Act, extending more representation to cities that had grown in population. The act also eliminated the so-called pocket boroughs, which were essentially phony towns that nevertheless sent representatives to Parliament. (The borough of Old Sarum, for example, boasted a population of a mere seven people—and yet sent two legislators to Parliament.)

The 1832 Reform Act extended voting rights to any man who could claim ownership of property with a value of at least ten pounds—a move that doubled the voting rolls from about two hundred thousand to about four hundred thousand. Reform-minded lawmakers pursued extending the voting franchise further, and by 1885 virtually all male Britons had been granted the right to vote and, therefore, the right to select their own members of Parliament. (Women were not granted suffrage until 1918—and even then, they had to be over age thirty to vote. The voting age for British women was finally lowered to twenty-one—equal to the minimum age for male voters—in 1928).

year-long war between France and England. After the English were ultimately defeated in 1214 at the Battle of Bouvines in France, England's King John imposed heavy taxes on the wealthy English barons in an effort to refill the royal treasury, which years of warfare had depleted.

Dismayed by this turn of events, in 1215 a group of these barons sought to limit the absolute authority of the English king. They drew up a charter, which they called the Magna Carta, a Latin term for "grand charter," and demanded that John accept it. When the king refused, the barons raised their own army, marched on London, and seized the city. Facing expulsion from the throne, John realized he had no choice but to agree to the barons' demands. On June 15 he affixed the royal seal to the Magna Carta, establishing the document as the written law of England.

In addition to limiting the authority of the British monarch, the Magna Carta created a judicial system and guaranteed fair trials to all free subjects. The document also created a royal council composed of barons and established a law forbidding the king to levy taxes without the council's consent. By 1236 the royal council was known by a new name—Parliament, a word that stems from the Latin term *parliamentum*, which translates literally to "discussion." Henceforth, under the authority first granted to it by the Magna Carta, Parliament became the lawmaking body of the English government. However, even though the Magna Carta established an important precedent by decreeing equal treatment for citizens under law and creating a lawmaking body, Parliament was hardly a truly representative government. With one brief exception during the rule of Earl Simon de Montfort from 1263 to 1264, for centuries membership in it was limited to the landed gentry.

The First American Laws

As Europe emerged from the medieval era, explorers sailed west and encountered the New World. Settlements were established in America; the first English colony was founded in 1607 in Jamestown, Virginia. At first the colonists resolved to live under English law, but it soon became apparent that the laws that had been effective in maintaining order in the civilized atmosphere of London society were not working in the Virginia wilderness. The colonists faced hunger, disease, and drought, and infighting soon erupted. A strong form of discipline was needed, and in 1610 a new governor, Thomas West, also known as Baron De La Warre, arrived in the colony, aiming to impose law and order.

West, along with two other colonists, Thomas Gates and Thomas Dale, wrote the Laws Divine, Moral and Martial, which West employed to govern the colony. The set of thirty-seven laws, spanning eighteen handwritten pages, established rules for the colonial society and dictated punishments for violators. These early written laws imposed on the subjects of the territory that would later become the world's first true democracy were hardly democratic—they required all colonists to attend church services twice a day, prohibited them from speaking ill of one another, and put the administration of justice entirely in the hands of the governor.

King John signs the Magna Carta in England in 1215. The document limited the king's authority, created a judicial system, guaranteed fair trials, and created a lawmaking body that became known as Parliament.

Moreover, the governor could impose the death penalty for infractions such as stealing chickens. Still, these harsh measures worked: Order was restored in Jamestown. In 1615 colonist Ralph Hamor attributed the survival of the colonists largely to the Laws Divine, Moral and Martial. Without them, he said, "I see not how the utter subversion and ruin of the Colony should have been prevented."[11]

The Mayflower Compact

A decade later and hundreds of miles north of Virginia, the colonists who had sailed to the New World aboard the *Mayflower* in pursuit of religious freedom anchored in Plymouth Bay, Massachusetts. After a harrowing two-month journey across the Atlantic Ocean in 1620, leaders of the Plymouth Colony feared that the harsh elements, disease, hunger, unfriendly native inhabitants, and dissent among the colonists could lead to disaster. They realized a set of laws would be vital to guide the colonists in their new surroundings, so while still aboard the ship, they drew up the Mayflower Compact.

Unlike the Laws Divine, Moral and Martial, the Mayflower Compact did not list specific regulations or penalties for infractions, but instead set up a framework under which the colonists, when they saw the need, would collectively decide upon whatever rules or laws they believed necessary to maintain order. Moreover, unlike the document that West imposed on the Jamestown colonists, the Mayflower Compact was written by the colonists themselves—giving them a voice in the laws under which they would live. Under the terms of the compact, the colonists would

> covenant and combine ourselves together into a civil body politic, for our better ordering and preservation, and furtherance of the ends aforesaid; and by virtue hereof enact, constitute and frame such just and equal laws, ordinances, acts, constitutions and offices, from time to time, as shall be thought most meet [fair] and convenient for the general good of the colony, under which we promise all due submission and obedience.[12]

Seeking a Solid Foundation

The Mayflower pilgrims were followed by others who established settlements in what later became Pennsylvania, New York, and Maryland, among other places. As these settlements grew into regional colonies, they formed representative governments—the Virginia House of Burgesses was first, convening in 1619.

Following the War of Independence, many political leaders in America realized that a tremendous opportunity was at hand: the chance to establish a new nation governed by a set of laws that would be truly democratic. In 1782 Alexander Hamilton, a New York lawyer who became an important voice in the drafting of the US Constitution, wrote, "Peace made . . . a new scene opens. The object then will be to make our independence a blessing. To do this we must secure our union on solid foundations."[13]

Hamilton, Madison, and the other leaders of the new nation had studied the shortcomings of the Roman senate, Parliament, and the early attempts at lawmaking in places like the Jamestown colony. As the delegates prepared for the 1787 Constitutional Convention, they aimed to forge a set of laws that, unlike those earlier attempts, would withstand the test of time.

Chapter 2

Crises in the New Nation

The signing of the Declaration of Independence and eventual surrender by the British at Yorktown firmly established the new nation: the United States of America. But when it came to deciding on a framework for a government or a set of laws to guide the new American society, the states were hardly united.

Soon after adoption of the Declaration of Independence, the Continental Congress turned its attention to establishing a central government and drafting a set of laws. The congress worked on the document—officially the Articles of Confederation and Perpetual Union, but known more familiarly as the Articles of Confederation—for four years, ratifying it less than a year before Cornwallis surrendered.

Essentially, the Articles specified that each state would maintain a spirit of independence, ensuring only that they would cooperate with one another to solve common problems. The Articles declared:

> Each state retains its sovereignty, freedom, and independence, and every power, jurisdiction, and right, which is not by this Confederation expressly delegated to the United States, in Congress assembled. The said States hereby severally enter into a firm league of friendship with each other, for their common defense, the security of their liberties, and their mutual and general welfare, binding themselves to assist each other, against all force offered to, or attacks made upon them, or any of them, on account of religion, sovereignty, trade, or any other pretense whatever.[14]

The Articles were intended to bind the colonies together during a time of war; following the war the Articles were clearly inadequate to maintain an effective federal government or ensure individual rights. The Articles provided the federal government with no power to levy taxes, raise an army to defend the country should a foreign or domestic threat arise, or regulate trade. The Articles also failed to provide the new federal government with the power to pay off its debts, which, at the conclusion of a six-year war, were considerable.

In fact, when it came to this issue, the new state legislatures were decidedly sluggish. Shortly after the war ended, the Continental Congress wrote the presidents of the thirteen state legislatures numerous times, asking the states to send money to the federal treasury to help pay off the war debts. Invariably, these pleas fell on deaf ears. Says Harvard University Law School professor Mark Roe, "After independence from Britain . . . America's states refused to repay their Revolutionary War debts. Some were unable; others were unwilling. The country as a whole operated as a loose confederation that . . . lacked taxing and other authority. It could not solve its financial problems."[15]

Call for a Convention

Following the war George Washington emerged as a major advocate for the establishment of a strong federal government as well as a set of laws that would define the powers of the government and the rights of citizens. "I do not conceive we can exist long as a nation without having lodged somewhere the power which will pervade the whole Union in as energetic manner as the authority of the state governments extends over the several states,"[16] he said. Washington was joined in this call by several political leaders of the era, including Alexander Hamilton, the New York lawyer who had served as a senior aide to Washington during the war; and James Madison, the owner of a Virginia tobacco plantation.

Hamilton was the first to call for the states to hold a convention with the sole purpose of drafting a constitution. He soon found himself working hard to convince others of his position. He wrote letters to influential friends and authored articles for newspapers, explaining his ideas. He

General Charles Cornwallis surrenders to victorious colonial troops at Yorktown in 1781. The signing of the Declaration of Independence, followed by the British surrender at the Battle of Yorktown, firmly established the new United States.

traveled throughout the states to make speeches and even persuaded the New York State Assembly to adopt a resolution endorsing the convention.

Hamilton's belief in the need for a Constitutional Convention ran counter to the opinions of other political leaders, who thought the Articles of Confederation conferred on Congress all the authority it needed to administer the federal government and that the states should continue to be largely independent of federal control. Pennsylvanian Samuel Bryan warned that a constitution would be the product of "wealthy and ambitious [men], who, in every community, think they have the right to lord it over their fellow creatures."[17]

Printing Continentals

Despite the initial opposition to a constitutional convention, however, a series of events in the first few years following the war convinced many political leaders that the state governments were incapable of solving the problems facing the new American society and that a strong federal presence would be desirable. For starters, one of the problems left over from the war was the rampant inflation that had swept through the new American economy.

Before the revolution, each colony issued its own paper currency—there were, for example, Pennsylvania pound notes, South Carolina pound notes, and Maryland pound notes. Moreover, from time to time the colonies would stop recognizing the value of paper money and authorize only transactions conducted in coins minted from silver and gold. And although the colonies recognized each other's currencies, they did not necessarily assign equal values to them. An anonymous English visitor traveling in the colonies in 1742 is said to have lamented, "There certainly can't be a greater Grievance to a Traveller, from one Colony to another, than the different values their Paper Money bears."[18]

When the war erupted, the Continental Congress became responsible for raising an army. With no power to impose taxes, the congress was forced to pay for the war by issuing its own paper money, known as continental currency, or continentals. "Congress issued the continentals because the states did not want to levy taxes to finance a war that was partially sparked by English taxation of the colonies,"[19] says Larry Allen, a professor of economics at Lamar University in Beaumont, Texas. Indeed, the states were saddled with their own debt—reluctant to levy taxes to fund their own militias and other wartime expenses, the states borrowed to pay their bills. When the war was over, the thirteen states owed some $25 million to creditors. In today's dollars, a debt of that size would total in the hundreds of millions of dollars.

America Defaults

To pay for the war, the Continental Congress employed a technique that desperate governments often still use to pay their debts: Whenever it needed more money to buy arms, ammunition, uniforms, or provisions for soldiers, it would simply order more money printed. Eventually, it approved the printing of continentals with face values totaling

$41 million. While this scheme usually helps solve immediate financial problems, in the long run it invariably causes what is known as inflation: Since the cash has little actual value to begin with, the more cash that is printed, the less it will buy. According to Allen, by 1779 continentals were worth a hundredth of their face value. By the end of the war, continentals were all but worthless.

This meant that American manufacturers, mill owners, shopkeepers, and farmers who had helped finance the war by accepting continentals in exchange for uniforms, arms, provisions, and other supplies were now holding notes of currency that were without real value. And not only Americans held worthless notes. During the war the Continental Congress had borrowed heavily from the government of France, Great Britain's longtime enemy, as well as from the governments of Spain and Holland. In fact, the congress borrowed $2 million from the French—the equivalent of hundreds of millions of dollars today.

Powerless to levy taxes or to compel the states to pay off the national debt, in 1785 the new American government defaulted, or failed to repay, its loans from France. A debt of such enormous size—and no resources to satisfy the lenders—could have a devastating impact on the future of the country. It would mean that American banks, as well as European ones, would be unlikely to lend money to the American government, hampering the new country's efforts to establish a capital city, finance public services, or raise an army should a new threat emerge.

In fact, a new threat did surface. And when it did, the Continental Congress found itself powerless to act.

Shays's Rebellion

In the years following the War of Independence, American commerce had been slow to recover. Many farmers and tradespeople borrowed heavily. By 1786 many farmers were losing their farms to creditors, who won court orders that enabled city and town governments to seize the properties and sell them at auctions to satisfy the debts. On August 29, 1786, court was set to convene in Northampton, Massachusetts. But before the court could open, an angry mob of farmers stormed the

"Not Worth a Continental"

The term "not worth a continental" was a familiar phrase uttered in American streets during and after the War of Independence. Even George Washington once said, "A wagonload of continentals will hardly purchase a wagonload of provisions."

In fact, people were suspicious of the currency printed by the Continental Congress from the outset, believing that since the congress lacked the power to tax and held no reserves of gold and silver in the national treasury, the continentals would be worthless. In an effort to enhance people's confidence in the notes, the congress hired patriots such as Benjamin Franklin and Paul Revere to print them. But even with Franklin and Revere vouching for the value of the continentals, many Americans were loath to accept them as payment for goods and services.

During the War of Independence, the British realized the havoc they could wreak on the American economy by flooding the colonies with counterfeit continentals. Many of these fake notes made it into circulation in America, further damaging the ability of the Continental Congress to fund the war.

Quoted in Federal Reserve Bank of San Francisco, "Colonial and Continental Currency: Initial Issue of the Continental Congress," 2012. www.frbsf.org.

courthouse and shut it down, prohibiting that day's business, during which a judge was expected to approve several seizures. The mob was led by a local farmer, Daniel Shays.

Shays and his followers called themselves Regulators; the name stemmed from their desire to "regulate" the government—in other words, impose their will on the government so judges could not sell farmers' properties. The Regulators placed a lot of the blame on wealthy merchants who had advanced them credit and were now calling in the loans by having farms and businesses seized. Regulators harassed these merchants by assaulting them, breaking into their shops and committing vandalism, and finding other ways to make mischief.

Soon, the tactics employed by Shays and his followers were copied in other Massachusetts towns. The movement gained popular support and later became known as Shays's Rebellion. Eventually, an estimated fifteen thousand Massachusetts farmers and others joined the uprising.

Bordering on Anarchy

Massachusetts governor James Bowdoin found his state powerless to put down the rebellion. He ordered the state's militia to track down Shays and other movement leaders, but militia members refused to take up arms against the farmers, because they sympathized with their plight.

The Massachusetts assembly reacted by passing a law giving local sheriffs the authority to shoot Regulators who blocked judges from signing seizure orders, but this action was largely ineffective because the sheriffs often sympathized with the Regulators. When the state government issued warrants for the arrest of the rebel leaders, posting bounties for their capture, vigilantes known as lighthorsemen rode into the countryside to capture the leaders and collect the rewards. These encounters usually led to skirmishes between the Regulators and lighthorsemen.

Three years after the end of the War of Independence, Massachusetts was in chaos as Regulators and their sympathizers ignored the law, barred judges from entering courthouses, and shot it out with the wild and unpredictable lighthorsemen. Said Manasseh Cutler, a minister from Boston, "We are in this commonwealth on the very border of complete anarchy."[20] Added Fisher Ames, a lawyer from the Massachusetts town of Dedham, "You will behold men who have ever been civilized, returning to barbarism, and threatening to become fiercer than the savage children of nature."[21]

Before the American Revolution every colony issued its own paper currency. Lacking authority to levy taxes, the Continental Congress had to print its own money to pay for the war. Pictured are currencies from New York (1); Connecticut (2); US Continental currency (3); Vermont (4); New Jersey (5); and North Carolina (6).

End of the Rebellion

Outside Massachusetts the uprising concerned political leaders who feared it could spread to other states and ultimately prompt them to leave the new union. The Continental Congress, lacking authority to raise an army, could offer no assistance—but it did ask a Massachusetts political leader, Henry Knox, to monitor the rebellion. Richard Henry Lee, a cavalry officer and friend of Washington, read Knox's reports and told Washington of his deep concern for the future of America. "The malcontents," Lee wrote to Washington, "[have as] their object . . . the abolition of debts, the division of property, and reunion with Great Britain. . . . In one word, my dear General, we are all in dire apprehension that a beginning of anarchy with its calamitys has approached."[22]

Eventually, Bowdoin appealed to wealthy Massachusetts landowners, who donated $20,000 to enable him to raise a private militia. Numbering some forty-four hundred soldiers, the militia encountered Shays and sixteen hundred of his followers on February 4, 1787, near the city of Springfield, where the rebels intended to capture an arsenal.

Although the militia managed to disperse the mob and capture many of the rebels, Shays and other rebel leaders fled to the still unsettled territory of Vermont. They were eventually tried in absentia for treason (meaning they were put on trial even though they had not been captured), convicted, and sentenced to hang. Among the people of Massachusetts, though, Shays and his allies were regarded as heroes. In 1789 Bowdoin's successor, John Hancock, issued pardons to the rebels. Those who had been captured and were in custody were freed.

Trade Disputes

Many political leaders believed Shays's Rebellion could have been ended much earlier had the federal government been endowed with the powers under law to address such threats to the security of the country. Moreover, Hamilton argued, Shays's Rebellion would never have occurred had the federal government been granted power to levy taxes. By refusing to impose taxes to pay off its war debts, Hamilton declared, Massachusetts had driven merchants to find other ways to recoup the financial losses they suffered by extending credit to the state during the war. And so these merchants went after the farmers who owed them money by seizing their lands. "If Shays had not been a desperate debtor, it is much to be doubted whether Massachusetts would have been plunged into civil war,"[23] wrote Hamilton.

These advocates found their opportunity to call for a national Constitutional Convention at a meeting that had been scheduled for September 1786 in Annapolis, Maryland. Twelve delegates from Virginia, Delaware, Pennsylvania, New Jersey, and New York attended the Annapolis Convention—at a time when Shays's Rebellion was still very much a threat to the peace of Massachusetts.

The Annapolis Convention had been called to address another crisis that was brewing in American society—one that the Continental Congress was, once again, powerless to resolve. Under the Articles of Confederation, the congress held no power to regulate trade among the states. As a result, the state assemblies set their own rules for interstate commerce, meaning they all adopted their own tariff laws—taxing crops and manufactured goods as they crossed state lines.

Friction Among the States

States enacted these laws to raise revenue for their treasuries. In Virginia, for example, ships docking in the state's ports were ordered to pay Virginia tariffs, and if their owners refused, the state reserved the right to seize the ships and their cargos. To enforce its tariff laws, Virginia—as did eight other states—maintained its own navy.

It did not take long for these tariffs to cause friction among the states. States found themselves in competition with one another for trade, and these tariffs often frustrated merchants attempting to trade across state lines. A New Jersey merchant, for example, may not have found it worthwhile to sell goods in Pennsylvania because of the cost of paying Pennsylvania's tariff.

Moreover, it was not unusual for one state to accuse another of unfair tactics to ensure that it got the upper hand in these trade wars. For example, Virginia and Maryland each laid claim to the right to navigate the Potomac River. Although navies from the two states stopped short of opening fire on one another, tempers often flared as political leaders from both sides found themselves unable to resolve the dispute.

The Annapolis Report

The Continental Congress had no power to resolve these disputes but believed that if delegates from the states were called together, they could find common ground and settle their differences. With this goal in mind, the congress asked the states to send delegates to the convention in Annapolis. As things turned out, the states seemed to have little enthusiasm for the convention. Since only five states sent delegates, the convention lacked a quorum—representatives from a majority of the states—and therefore did not have the authority to set policies that would affect all thirteen states.

But the delegates to the convention—among them Madison and Hamilton—firmly believed that a much broader convention should be held, one that should deal with more than simple trade disputes. As a result, the delegates elected not to address the trade tariffs but rather to use the session to call for a meeting of state delegations in which a new national constitution would be drawn up to replace the Articles of Confederation. Says historian Richard Beeman, "They intended to scrap the Articles of Confederation altogether, create an entirely new government in its place, and, in the process, effect a dramatic change in the balance of power between the central government and those of the individual states."[24]

Their findings, titled the Annapolis Report, were written by Hamilton. The report urged the congress "with the utmost deference to devise such further provisions as should appear to them necessary to render the constitution of the federal government adequate to the exigencies [urgent needs] of the union."[25]

A New Framework for Governance

The Continental Congress received the report at the same time Shays's Rebellion was threatening to plunge Massachusetts into a full-fledged civil war and spread to other states. The congress debated the findings of the Annapolis Convention for the remainder of 1786 and into the early weeks of 1787. Finally, in February 1787, just a few days after Bowdoin's private militia broke up Shays's Rebellion, the congress ap-

The Fate of Daniel Shays

After fleeing to Vermont, Daniel Shays won a pardon from Massachusetts governor John Hancock but returned only briefly to his home state. Shays eventually settled in the town of Sparta, New York, where he lived out his life.

There Shays lived next door to a young man who worked as an apprentice in a local mill. Shays struck up a friendship with the apprentice, whose name was Millard Fillmore. In 1850 Fillmore took office as the thirteenth president of the United States. In his memoirs, Fillmore recalls meeting Shays and expresses surprise that his neighbor was the infamous leader of Shays's Rebellion. "He seemed to me a very common man and I could but wonder how he had become so famous, for it was as common when I was a boy to hurrah for Shays as it has been to hurrah for [Andrew] Jackson," wrote Fillmore.

In 1820 Shays was awarded a pension for his service in the War of Independence. He used his pension to buy a farm and small house outside Sparta. He died in 1825 at age seventy-eight.

Millard Fillmore, *Millard Fillmore Papers*. Buffalo, NY: Buffalo Historical Society, 1907, p. 387.

proved a resolution to hold a convention in Philadelphia in May for the purpose of authoring a new body of laws—a constitution for the United States.

The resolution hardly spoke to the enormity of the task that lay ahead for the convention delegates; it stated the gathering would be held "for the sole and express purpose of revising the Articles of Confederation, and reporting to Congress and the several legislatures such alterations and provisions therein as shall when agreed to in Congress and confirmed by the States, render the federal Constitution adequate to the exigencies of Government and the preservation of the Union."[26]

Despite the misgivings of several members of the congress who continued to believe the states should remain largely independent, evidence that the Articles of Confederation failed to provide an effective framework for governance was obvious. The country was in debt, unable to pay its creditors for a war that had ended some four years earlier. Inflation was out of control. Rebellion had broken out in Massachusetts. And trade disputes were causing conflict among several states. With those problems and many others to solve, the delegates selected to represent their states at the convention in Philadelphia girded themselves for the awesome task ahead.

Chapter 3

A Summer in Philadelphia

Fifty-five delegates traveled to Philadelphia to participate in the Constitutional Convention, which met in the Pennsylvania State House, headquarters of the state's assembly. The oldest delegate was Benjamin Franklin, the Philadelphia printer, inventor, and statesman who was eighty-one when the convention convened. The youngest was twenty-seven-year-old Jonathan Dayton of New Jersey.

George Washington attended as well, serving as a delegate from Virginia and agreeing to preside over the convention. Throughout the summer months, he stayed largely silent during the debates, but through the power of his personality, Washington could be counted on to issue calming words to ensure civility and provide guidance to the delegates.

Other delegates were well known in political circles: Alexander Hamilton was a member of the New York delegation; James Madison represented Virginia. Elbridge Gerry, a delegate from Massachusetts, represented his state, as did Rufus King, regarded as one of the leading orators of the era. In addition to Franklin, the Pennsylvania delegation included Thomas Mifflin, also a member of the Continental Congress and, later, a governor of his state.

Conspicuous by their absence were any delegates from Rhode Island, where the state assembly was controlled by politicians who vehemently opposed handing more powers to a central government and so refused to send representatives from their state. This attitude infuriated Washington, among others. "Rhode Island," he declared, "still perseveres in the impolitic—unjust—and one might add without much impropriety scandalous conduct, which seems to have marked all her councils of late."[27] Added Madison, "Nothing can exceed the wickedness and folly which continue to reign there."[28]

The Virginia Plan

The other states were far more enthusiastic than Rhode Island; nevertheless, the convention hardly got off to a running start when it opened on May 14, 1787. Only two delegations were on hand that day—those representing Virginia and Pennsylvania. Over the next two weeks, most of the other delegates drifted into town. Some delegates, however, did not make it to Philadelphia until later that summer. The first two of New Hampshire's four delegates did not arrive until late July because the state needed time to raise money to pay for their trip.

Finally, though, on May 29 the delegates started their serious work. The original mandate issued by the Continental Congress called for the convention to revise the Articles of Confederation, making them more responsive to the problems faced by American society. But the delegates soon decided to toss out the Articles and draft a completely new document.

On the first day of debate, Edmund Randolph, the governor of Virginia, proposed abandoning the Articles of Confederation. He argued that they had been written at a time when the current problems facing America did not yet exist—there were no trade disputes dividing the states, no rebellion had broken out in Massachusetts, and no foreign debts were due.

Randolph then proposed the Virginia Plan, an early draft of the Constitution authored by Madison. The Virginia Plan provided for two lawmaking bodies, including a House of Representatives and a Senate; a chief executive, who would be charged with implementing the laws; and a third branch, the judiciary, charged with interpreting laws and ensuring they were applied equally to all citizens.

After much disagreement and debate, delegates to the Constitutional Convention—among them George Washington, Benjamin Franklin, and Thomas Jefferson—sign the Constitution in 1787. The document was then sent to the states for ratification.

Defending States' Rights

Under the Virginia Plan, the House and Senate would propose and adopt legislation to address national problems the states were unable to solve through their own laws. A main tenet held that members of the new House and Senate would be elected directly by the people rather than appointed by their state governments, as members of the Continental Congress had been under the Articles of Confederation. Moreover, according to Madison's early draft, the states were not granted equal representation in the two legislative bodies, as they were guaranteed in the Continental Congress under the Articles. Instead, representation would be based on "the number of free inhabitants"[29]—in other words, the population—of each state.

The Virginia Plan was not received with overwhelming enthusiasm. Many of the delegates still believed in states' rights and feared Madison's plan granted the federal government far too much authority. William Paterson, a delegate from New Jersey, complained, "If the Confederacy was radically wrong, let us return to our states and obtain larger powers, not assume them of ourselves. . . . We have no power to vary the idea of equal sovereignty."[30] Even Randolph conceded the Virginia Plan would create "a strong consolidated union in which the idea of the states should be annihilated."[31]

The First US Presidents

Although George Washington is commonly known as the first president of the United States, there were, in fact, eight men who held the office of chief executive before he was elected under the terms of the US Constitution in 1788. Under the Articles of Confederation, the chief executive was known as the President of the United States in Congress Assembled, and the Congress was given the authority to "appoint one of their members to preside, provided that no person be allowed to serve in the office of president more than one year in any term of three years." The president's chief responsibility was to chair sessions of Congress—fearful that the president would assume the powers of a monarch, the Continental Congress reserved virtually all powers for itself.

The eight men who held the position were John Hanson of Maryland; Elias Boudinot, Thomas Mifflin, and Arthur St. Clair of Pennsylvania; John Hancock and Nathaniel Gorham of Massachusetts; and Richard Henry Lee and Cyrus Griffin of Virginia. Griffin was the last president to serve under the terms of the Articles of Confederation, stepping down when Washington was inaugurated in 1789.

Quoted in Yale School of Law, "Articles of Confederation," 2008. http://avalon.law.yale.edu.

A Deadlocked Convention

The delegates who feared the Constitution would create a federal government endowed with unfettered powers endorsed a competing plan, known as the New Jersey Plan, drawn up by Paterson. Paterson suggested Congress be given the power to regulate interstate commerce and levy taxes but each state be limited to one vote in Congress. Moreover, Paterson suggested the chief executive be appointed by Congress rather than elected by the people.

Debate over the two plans raged into July. Delegates from smaller states fretted their states would lack influence in Congress if the larger states dominated the two chambers. Delegates from the larger states questioned whether a tiny state, such as Connecticut, should be entitled to membership in Congress equal to that of a large state, such as Virginia. The delegates seemed deadlocked, and many talked of ending the convention and going home. Even Washington expressed concern the convention would fail, writing to a friend, "Everybody wishes, everybody expects something from the convention; but what will be the final result of its deliberations, the book of fate must disclose."[32]

On the morning of July 4, the convention opened to the sound of booming cannons. It was Independence Day. Nearby, the delegates heard thirteen shots fired—one for each state. Eleven years before, the Declaration of Independence had been signed in the same building in which the new nation's constitution was stalled over representation in Congress.

Memories of what had occurred on July 4, 1776, may have stirred many of the delegates—who were also signers of the Declaration of Independence—into a mood for compromise. One of these was Franklin, who aimed to broker a deal.

The Great Compromise

To break the deadlock, Franklin, along with the aid of John Dickinson of Delaware and Roger Sherman of Connecticut, proposed what was known as the Great Compromise or the Connecticut Compromise.

Under the plan, representation in the House would be based on population; as for the Senate, each state would be entitled to send two members to the legislative body.

Delegates from some of the larger states were still not satisfied, though. They feared the smaller states could band together in the Senate to form political blocs, controlling legislation in the Congress. And so Franklin crafted another compromise: He proposed all legislative matters concerning financial issues originate in the House. Since membership in the House would be based on population, the compromise meant the states with the largest populations—and therefore the most taxpayers—would hold most of the power in Congress when it came to deciding how money would be raised and spent by the federal government.

Until then, Franklin had not played too active a role in the convention—he was frail and ailing from gout and bladder stones. But his presence was still very much felt in the Pennsylvania State House. Working behind the scenes throughout the summer, Franklin had often invited delegates to his home for tea, building friendships with them. At one point he counseled some stubborn delegates, "Declarations of a fixed opinion, and, of determined resolution never to change it, neither enlighten nor convince us. Positiveness and warmth on one side, naturally beget their like on the other."[33]

Now Franklin made use of the relationships he had sown that summer, using his enormous influence to sell the Great Compromise to the other delegates. On July 16 the convention voted to accept the compromise. Says Franklin biographer Walter Isaacson:

Franklin's role . . . was crucial. He embodied the spirit and issued the call for compromise, he selected the most palatable option available and refined it, and he wrote the motion and picked the right time to offer it. His prestige, neutrality, and his eminence made it easier for all to swallow. The artisan had taken a little from all sides and made a joint good enough to hold together a nation for centuries.[34]

The Three-Fifths Compromise

Although most of the delegates accepted the Great Compromise, many did so with considerable trepidation due to one aspect of the plan. Indeed, the issue that concerned them during that summer in 1787 continued to be a concern to many people well after the close of the convention, eventually dominating—and dividing—American society over the next eight decades. That issue was slavery.

Slaves captured from Africa first stepped onto American soil in 1619 to labor on the plantations of the Jamestown colony. By the time of the convention, slavery was very much a part of American society. In 1787 some six hundred thousand people—a number representing nearly 20 percent of the people residing in America—were owned by other people.

Although there were many abolitionists in the room, the abolitionist cause was given little debate that summer in the Pennsylvania State House. At the time the only state where slavery was outlawed was Massachusetts. Most slaves lived in the southern states, and delegates from the northern states knew that without the support of the delegates from the South, the Constitution would never be ratified.

One of the few delegates to call for abolition was Maryland representative Luther Martin, who decried the hypocrisy of writing a body of laws to ensure equal rights for Americans while leaving hundreds of thousands in bondage. He declared, "Slaves weakened one part of the Union which the other parts were bound to protect."[35] Other delegates took a more pragmatic view. Oliver Ellsworth, a representative from Connecticut, reminded the delegates that slave labor helped keep prices low in the northern states for cotton goods and other crops harvested in the South. "What enriches a part enriches the whole," Ellsworth said, "and the states are the best judges of their particular interest."[36]

Ultimately, rather than debating the morality of slavery, the delegates focused on whether slaves could be regarded as full citizens for the purposes of calculating a state's population. This was a significant issue because representation in the House would be based on population. Therefore, delegates from the South pressed hard for slaves to be counted as free men and women.

Ultimately, the delegates agreed to the Three-Fifths Compromise— to count slaves as three-fifths of a free man or woman, therefore giving the southern states increased representation in the House based on their slave populations. Without the Three-Fifths Compromise, conceded Hamilton, "no union could possibly have been formed."[37]

Responding to the Three-Fifths Compromise, Martin complained, "[Slavery is] inconsistent with the principles of the revolution and dishonorable to the American character to have such a feature in the Constitution."[38] Later that summer he refused to sign the Constitution.

Victory for States' Rights

The northern states did win one important concession from the South on the slavery issue. The delegates agreed to provide the federal government with the power to regulate interstate commerce. Under the terms of their compromise with the northern delegates, the southern states agreed slaves would be regarded as any other property imported and sold in the United States. Therefore, Congress would not have the power to determine whether slavery was legal or illegal but would reserve the power to levy tariffs on the importation of slaves as well as impose taxes on their sale. In fact, article 1 of the Constitution levies a tariff of ten dollars per slave brought into the country.

Moreover, the southern states agreed to voluntarily cease importation of slaves until 1808. After ratification, Congress voted to permanently ban the importation of slaves, beginning in 1808.

Essentially, the Three-Fifths Compromise represented a victory for the states' rights advocates at the convention because it reserved for the states the authority to determine the legality of slavery. "The question before the convention was not, 'Shall slavery be abolished?'" says historian Catherine Drinker Bowen. "It was rather, 'Who shall have the power to control it—states or the national government?' As the Constitution now stood, Congress could control the traffic in slaves exactly as it controlled all other trade and commerce."[39]

The first African slaves arrive in North America in 1619. The issue of slavery divided delegates taking part in the Constitutional Convention.

Coequal Branches of Government

The debate over the Great Compromise illustrates how much of the convention was devoted to the powers and limitations of Congress, the lawmaking body created under the Constitution. Under the Virginia Plan, the Constitution would also establish a chief executive and judiciary.

Rhode Island's Refusal

Rhode Island was the lone state that refused to send members to the Constitutional Convention. The reason lay in the makeup of the state: Then as now, citizens of the smallest state in the union, Rhode Islanders were fiercely independent and suspicious of the motivations of the other states. Following the War of Independence, Rhode Islanders found their state in deep debt, with few resources to repay it. They worried a powerful federal government would impose new tax burdens on them.

Still, Rhode Islanders were not unanimous in their opposition to the Constitution. Pro-Constitution advocates in the state assembly did manage to force three votes in the legislature on a motion to send delegates to the convention. All three failed, however. In addition, members of the Rhode Island delegation to the Continental Congress urged their state assembly to participate in the convention, but their pleas fell on deaf ears. Several prominent merchants appealed to the assembly to send delegates, but they were ignored as well.

Through it all, most Rhode Island political leaders stood steadfast in opposition to the Constitutional Convention. In answering one critic, Governor John Collins said:

> Our conduct has been reprobated by the illiberal, and many severe and unjust sarcasms propagated against us; but, sir, when we state to you the reason, and evince the cause, the liberal mind will be convinced that we were actuated by the greater principle which hath ever been characteristic of this state—the love of true constitutional liberty, and the fear we have of making innovations on the rights and liberties of the citizens at large.

Quoted in Benjamin F. Shearer, *The United States: Oklahoma to Wyoming.* Westport, CT: Greenwood, 2004, p. 1,057.

The powers and responsibilities of these two branches were also subjected to heated debate, with the delegates ultimately deciding that the chief executive, or president, and the judiciary would be co-equal branches of government along with Congress. As such, the three branches would provide checks and balances on one another's roles.

Madison's Virginia Plan called for the chief executive to be selected by the legislature in the same fashion in which the prime minister of Great Britain is chosen by the members of the majority party in Parliament. Eventually, Madison changed his mind, deciding that such a system would not lend itself to making the presidency a coequal branch of government. A president selected by the Congress, Madison concluded, would owe a debt to Congress and could not be counted on to act independently.

Veto Power

To ensure Congress could not usurp the power of the president, the delegates provided for the election of the chief executive through the Electoral College, a body that would cast votes for the president based on the popular votes cast in the states. Therefore, Congress would have no role in selecting the president who would, therefore, enjoy independence from Congress. And to provide further checks and balances on the president and Congress, the delegates gave the president veto power over legislation but also provided Congress with the means to override presidential vetoes.

Pennsylvania delegate James Wilson was the convention's leading advocate for providing Congress with this ability, arguing that it was necessary to ensure the president could not grow more powerful than Congress. "Without such a defense," he argued, "the legislature can at any moment sink into non-existence."[40] Under the terms provided in the Constitution, Congress can negate a presidential veto of legislation by mustering a two-thirds vote to override.

The courts were also guaranteed independence. Under article 3, the Constitution provides for a Supreme Court and lower courts, giving them sole authority to mete out justice, thereby ensuring the president could not seize power in the mode of a European monarch, throwing enemies into prison without trial. Also, the Constitution forbids Congress from cutting the salary of a judge—a protection the delegates regarded as important, believing unscrupulous lawmakers could get rid of judges they objected to by refusing to pay them.

Necessary and Proper

Having established a framework for government as well as defined the roles of the three branches of government, the delegates turned to more practical matters. The war debts were still very much a concern, and following Shays's Rebellion, the delegates were well aware of the need for the federal government to respond to emergencies. And so the delegates endowed Congress with the authority to levy and collect taxes, thereby raising money to outfit an army, pay off the national debt, and provide whatever services the government felt inclined to provide to the American people. These provisions meant the federal government now possessed powers that had been denied the Continental Congress under the Articles of Confederation.

This authority was included under what is known as the Necessary and Proper Clause of the Constitution. Several delegates, led by Randolph, called for specific duties of the federal government to be outlined in the Constitution—such as the power to make treaties, raise an army, operate a postal service, coin money, and so on. Randolph's group was opposed by a faction led by Wilson, who proposed instead that the Constitution provide the federal government with more general powers. Eventually, these delegates prevailed, and a clause was written into the Constitution giving Congress the power "to make Laws that shall be necessary and proper for carrying into execution the foregoing powers, and all other powers vested by this Constitution in the government of the United States, or in any department or officer thereof." The Necessary and Proper Clause endowed Congress with enormous power over the lives of Americans, giving lawmakers the authority to adopt legislation, and raise money through taxes, for virtually any purpose they deemed necessary.

The Convention Adjourns

As the summer drew to a close, the delegates completed their work by providing a process under which the Constitution would be ratified, determining that it would take nine of the thirteen states to approve the document. The delegates also devised a process for amending the Constitution, establishing that amendments must be approved by three-quarters of the states.

One of the final pieces of business was to write the Preamble. The job fell to Gouverneur Morris, a delegate from Pennsylvania and a member of the Committee of Style and Arrangement, which had been appointed by the delegates to render the Constitution into written form. Morris's Preamble set the tone for the words that would follow. It reads:

> We the people of the United States, in Order to form a more perfect Union, establish Justice, insure domestic Tranquility, provide for the common defence, promote the general Welfare, and secure the Blessings of Liberty to ourselves and our Posterity, do ordain and establish this Constitution for the United States of America.

On September 17, 1787, their business concluded, thirty-nine of the fifty-five delegates placed their signatures on the Constitution and adjourned. It had been a long summer that had gotten off to a rocky start. But the delegates had overcome many obstacles—among them, Rhode Island's refusal to participate, the deadlock over representation in the House and Senate, the thorny issue of how to count the slaves, and the importance of providing checks and balances on the three co-equal branches of government.

Now, the nation had a body of laws the delegates believed would put American society on a firm footing for centuries to come. The delegates headed home, tasked now with the job of convincing their state assemblies to ratify their work.

Chapter 4

The Road to Ratification

Even as the delegates met in Philadelphia, a vocal Anti-Federalist movement had grown, composed of political leaders and other influential Americans who called for things to remain as they were—with most political power held by the states. They feared the Constitution authorized a concentration of power into the hands of just a few officials—the president, leaders of Congress, and the members of the Supreme Court.

Such a system, known as an oligarchy, was to their thinking too similar to the style of governance practiced by the European monarchs and aristocrats. In an October 16, 1787, letter to Edmund Randolph, Richard Henry Lee declared: "It cannot be denied with truth that this new constitution is, in its first principles, highly dangerous and oligarchic; and it is a point agreed that a government of the few is, of all governments, the worst."[41]

One major component of the proposed Constitution that concerned the Anti-Federalists was the Supremacy Clause, found in article 6. The clause reads, "The Constitution, and the Laws of the United States which shall be made in Pursuance thereof; and all Treaties made, or which shall be made, under the Authority of the United States, shall be the supreme Law of the Land." The clause means state laws could be superseded by federal laws, negating the intentions of state legislators. Says Stanford University historian Jack N. Rakove, "Anti-Federalists sensed that the supremacy clause of a written, popularly ratified constitution could indeed sweep aside all prior claims of rights and authority. The multiple sources for the authority of rights that the colonists had once invoked now seemed obsolete because the Constitution would create its own self-sufficient standards of legality."[42]

Moreover, Anti-Federalists demanded that basic rights be guaranteed under the Constitution. In fact, in his letter to Randolph, Lee referred to his desire to see a "bill of rights"[43] written into the document. Anti-Federalists reasoned that if the Constitution contained a Supremacy Clause, that clause should be applied to guarantee Americans would not be denied basic human rights by an oligarchic federal government.

Freedom of the Press

Many of these rights had been part of the fabric of American society since the growth of the colonies a century before. These rights included the right to assembly, or the right to gather to voice political views, and freedom of speech, or the right to express one's views in public without fear of reprisal from those in power. Another basic right claimed by Americans was the right to petition the government for redress of grievances—in other words, the right to ask for a law to be enacted or amended to correct a deficiency of society.

One of the most fundamental rights Americans came to expect was freedom of the press. Even in the eighteenth century, the press was an important institution in American life. Newspapers not only reported the news but also aired opinions about politics and American culture written by editors and other contributors to the marketplace of ideas of the eighteenth century. By contrast, in Europe freedom of the press was virtually unheard of—editors who printed opinions contrary to the liking of the monarch or an influential aristocrat could find themselves tossed into jail and their presses seized.

The expectation that the press in America was free to report the news and print opinions without fear of censorship by the government dates back to the colonial era. In 1732 a new royal governor, William Cosby, arrived in New York intending to rule the colony with an iron fist. Cosby imposed high taxes on landowners, rigged local elections, and appointed his friends to important jobs in the government.

Soon he found these activities criticized in a newspaper, the *New York Weekly Journal*, published by John Peter Zenger. Cosby endured Zenger's attacks for a time, but on December 3, 1733, when the *Journal* accused the governor of barring opponents from local city council meetings and permitting French warships to spy on the colony from New York Harbor, Cosby had Zenger arrested. He ordered his prosecutors to charge Zenger with "printing and publishing several seditious libels"[44]—in other words, lies meant to stir up treason against the government.

Land of Free Ideas

When Zenger came to trial in 1735, he discovered his lawyer had been appointed by Cosby—proof the royal governor intended to ensure the outcome of the proceedings. Another lawyer was in the room that day, though. Andrew Hamilton—a friend of Benjamin Franklin's—had been summoned to New York from Philadelphia by Zenger's allies to defend him against Cosby's style of justice. Hamilton announced he would now be representing Zenger. With the assent of the judges hearing the case, Cosby's handpicked lawyer stepped aside.

Hamilton never denied Zenger's newspaper printed the information about Cosby—instead, he argued publishing the stories was not a crime because they were true. "I hope it is not our bare printing or publishing a paper that will make it a libel," Hamilton told the jury. "You will have something more to do before you make my client a libeler. For the words themselves must be libelous—that is, false, malicious, and seditious—or else we are not guilty."[45]

Moreover, in making his closing argument to the jury, Hamilton called on the jurors to acquit his client because a verdict of guilty would send the message America was not a land of free ideas but instead a place where the government could use its power to stifle speech and censor the press. He told the jurors, "By an impartial and incorrupt verdict [you would lay] a noble foundation for securing to ourselves, our posterity and our neighbors that which nature and the laws of our country have given us a right—the liberty—both of exposing and opposing arbitrary power . . . by speaking, and writing, the truth."[46]

The jury returned a verdict of not guilty—establishing freedom of the press as a fundamental right of Americans. However, some five decades after the *Zenger* verdict was returned, the Anti-Federalists feared that this right would disappear under the new US Constitution.

The Federalist Papers

And so, in the months following the Constitutional Convention, as state assemblies started debating the merits of the Constitution, the Anti-Federalists campaigned against ratification. Among the ranks of the Anti-Federalists were many influential Americans, including signers of the Declaration of Independence, veterans of the Continental army, governors of states, and powerful members of state assemblies. Patrick Henry, one of the firebrands of the American Revolution and later a governor of Virginia, was vehemently opposed to ratification. Henry was an ardent believer in states' rights and feared the Constitution lessened

Patrick Henry addresses the Virginia Assembly at the dawn of the revolution. Several years later, Henry forcefully urged the members of the assembly to reject the Constitution because he feared it would lessen the authority of the states.

the authority of the states. He called on Virginia's assembly to reject the Constitution. Declared Henry, "[Virginians] called on us for liberty—called on us from our beloved endearments, which, from long habits, we were taught to revere. . . . On this awful occasion did you want a federal government? Did federal ideas lead you to the most splendid victories?"[47]

Supporters of the Constitution were clearly concerned that the oratory of Henry and the other Anti-Federalists would carry sway and that the document would fall short of adoption by the minimum required nine states. "Mr. Henry," James Madison told Thomas Jefferson, "is the great adversary who will render the event precarious. He is, I find, with his usual address working up every possible interest into a spirit of opposition."[48]

To counter the campaign waged by the Anti-Federalists, Madison, Hamilton, and a third proponent of the Constitution, John Jay, turned to their pens, authoring a series of eighty-five essays known as the Federalist Papers. Published between October 1787 and May 1788, the Federalist Papers were printed primarily in New York newspapers because New York State was believed to be one of the key "swing" states in the battle for ratification. Many newspapers in other areas also printed the essays, however, and in 1788, after the final essay was published, bound editions of the Federalist Papers were distributed throughout America.

The essays did not appear under the names of the authors but rather the pseudonym "Publius," the Latin term for "public." In them, Madison, Hamilton, and Jay explained the provisions of the Constitution, hoping to allay the fears that had been stoked by the Anti-Federalists. In Federalist No. 1, Hamilton laid the groundwork for the arguments that he and his coauthors intended to make—specifically that ratification of the Constitution represented the sole hope to rescue the union. Published on October 27, 1787, and addressed to the people of New York State, Federalist No. 1 opened with these words:

After an unequivocal experience of the inefficacy of the subsisting federal government, you are called upon to deliberate on a new Constitution for the United States of America. The subject speaks its own importance; comprehending in its consequences nothing less than the existence of the Union, the safety and welfare of the parts of which it is composed, the fate of an empire in many respects the most interesting in the world. It has been frequently remarked that it seems to have been reserved to the people of this country, by their conduct and example, to decide the important question, whether societies of men are really capable or not of establishing good government from reflection and choice, or whether they are forever destined to depend for their political constitutions on accident and force. If there be any truth in the remark, the crisis at which we are arrived may with propriety be regarded as the era in which that decision is to be made; and a wrong election of the part we shall act may, in this view, deserve to be considered as the general misfortune of mankind.[49]

"A Firm Union"

The Federalist Papers sought to forecast what could occur should the state assemblies reject the Constitution. The authors discussed the jealousies and suspicions that often pitted state against state. They predicted that without a strong national government in place, the union would be in danger of breaking apart, opening the way for the return of the British. Writing in Federalist No. 2, Jay declared, "This country and this people seem to have been made for each other, and it appears as if it was the design of Providence, that an inheritance so proper and convenient for a band of brethren, united to each other by the strongest ties, should never be split into a number of unsocial, jealous, and alien sovereignties."[50]

The essays defended the work of the Constitutional Convention, arguing that the crises leading to the convention—the enormous national debt, the trade disputes among the states, and the likelihood of a new insurrection—had been addressed in the Articles of the Constitution that the delegates in Philadelphia had debated and signed.

Addressing the bickering among the states, in Federalist No. 9 Hamilton compared the situation to the constant warfare that plagued the city-states of ancient Greece as well as the internal strife that eventually helped bring down the Roman republic. He wrote:

> A firm union will be of the utmost moment to the peace and liberty of the States, as a barrier against domestic faction and insurrection. It is impossible to read the history of the petty republics of Greece and Italy without feeling sensations of horror and disgust at the distractions with which they were continually agitated, and at the rapid succession of revolutions by which they were kept in a state of perpetual vibration between the extremes of tyranny and anarchy.[51]

Ratification Achieved

As the proponents of the Constitution and the Anti-Federalists presented their arguments, state assemblies started meeting for ratification votes. Delaware became the first state to ratify, approving the Constitution on December 6, 1787. Pennsylvania ratified on December 12, followed by New Jersey ten days later. Ratification next succeeded in Georgia, Connecticut, and Massachusetts.

The next state to vote was Rhode Island, where the Constitution's supporters suffered a setback. On March 24, 1788, the Rhode Island Assembly, still steadfastly wary of the intentions of the larger states, rejected the Constitution by a decisive majority.

A month later, the struggle for ratification appeared to be drawing to a close when Maryland voted to ratify. Ratification passed next in South Carolina. On June 21, New Hampshire ratified the Constitution, providing the ninth state needed to make the document the national law. Virginia and New York soon provided the tenth and eleventh votes.

In cities and towns across the country, people flocked to the streets to celebrate. The grandest celebration was held in Philadelphia, where

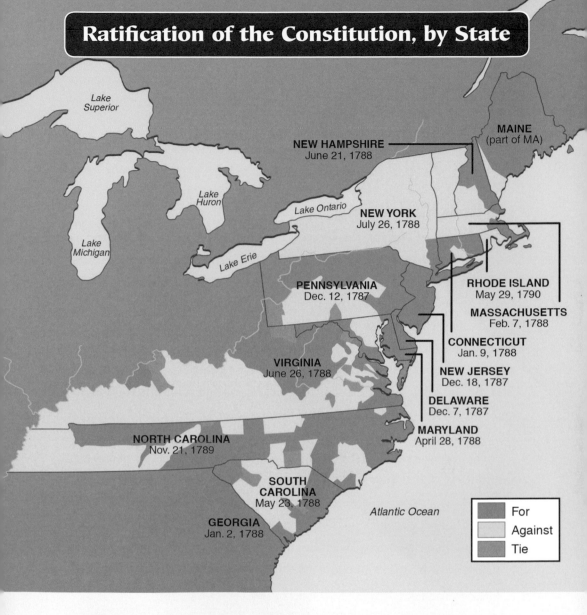

Ratification of the Constitution, by State

Lake Superior

Lake Huron

Lake Ontario

Lake Michigan

Lake Erie

MAINE
(part of MA)

NEW HAMPSHIRE
June 21, 1788

NEW YORK
July 26, 1788

PENNSYLVANIA
Dec. 12, 1787

RHODE ISLAND
May 29, 1790

MASSACHUSETTS
Feb. 7, 1788

CONNECTICUT
Jan. 9, 1788

VIRGINIA
June 26, 1788

NEW JERSEY
Dec. 18, 1787

DELAWARE
Dec. 7, 1787

NORTH CAROLINA
Nov. 21, 1789

MARYLAND
April 28, 1788

SOUTH CAROLINA
May 23, 1788

GEORGIA
Jan. 2, 1788

Atlantic Ocean

For
Against
Tie

at sunrise on Independence Day, a peal of bells rang out from the steeple at Christ Church and ships anchored in the city's harbor blasted their cannons. A parade was staged, and two ships, the *Federal Constitution* and the *Union*, were hoisted onto wagons and towed down city streets. All the vessels in the harbor were decorated in patriotic colors, as were many horses, wagons, and buildings in the city.

No parades commemorating ratification were held in Rhode Island or North Carolina. Unlike Rhode Island, where the Constitution was rejected outright, the North Carolina Assembly adjourned without taking a ratification vote. Both North Carolina and Rhode Island reconvened their assemblies a year later, each voting for ratification and joining the union—months after the first president elected under the terms of the Constitution, George Washington, took office.

Unfinished Business

The business of writing the Constitution was not, however, quite finished. To appease the Anti-Federalists, proponents for adoption promised that after ratification Congress would debate amendments to the Constitution for the purpose of framing a Bill of Rights.

The first members of the House of Representatives and Senate were elected in 1788 and took office in early 1789. Meeting in Philadelphia, the new lawmakers immediately got down to business. On September 25 Congress sent the first constitutional amendments to the state legislatures for ratification. The ten amendments that were ratified compose the Bill of Rights.

The First Amendment ensures religious tolerance in America, mandating that Congress could not establish a state-sanctioned religion. Many of the early settlers—among them the Puritans of Massachusetts and Quakers of Pennsylvania—came to America because they had been persecuted in Europe for their religious beliefs. By guaranteeing religious freedom, the First Amendment established the principle of separation of church and state, holding that Congress and all other aspects of American government would not be guided by religious doctrines. The First Amendment also guarantees freedom of the press, freedom of speech, the right of assembly, and the right of the people to petition Congress for redress of grievances—to seek new laws to correct the ills of society.

The next two amendments also spoke to individual rights. The Second Amendment guarantees the rights of the states to establish militias for self-protection. It also guarantees the people the "right to keep and bear Arms"—the right to own guns. The Third Amendment traces its

James Madison and Alexander Hamilton

The Constitution's two most ardent supporters, Alexander Hamilton and James Madison, each went on to serve their country after ratification. Madison was elected the nation's fourth president, serving two terms from 1809 to 1817.

During Madison's term the War of 1812 erupted between the United States and Great Britain. The war was caused by Great Britain's interference in American trade as well as the impressment of American sailors into the British navy. (British naval ships halted American merchant vessels on the high seas and kidnapped sailors, forcing them to serve aboard British ships.) In 1814 the war ended when the Treaty of Ghent was signed in Belgium, although neither side could claim a true military victory. Madison lived for another nineteen years after leaving office; he remained active in politics and public causes, helping to found the University of Virginia.

Hamilton, who had been a top aide to George Washington during the War of Independence, was appointed the nation's first secretary of the treasury in 1789. As the nation's chief financial officer, Hamilton was responsible for rescuing the country from the enormous debt it faced following the war. He shepherded measures through Congress that enabled the federal government to collect taxes and sell bonds to investors. He died after helping engineer the defeat of a political rival, Aaron Burr, who had been campaigning for governor of New York. An embittered Burr challenged Hamilton to a duel. Hamilton accepted, and on July 12, 1804, Burr shot Hamilton to death.

roots to the era following the French and Indian War, when the British government ordered colonists to house troops in their homes. It prohibits the quartering of troops in private homes without the owners' consent.

Protections Against Unfair Trials

The next five amendments concentrate on the rights guaranteed to individuals in courts of law—places where citizens of European countries were often subjected to phony trials, biased testimony, and judgments based on the whims of monarchs and aristocrats. In the Fourth Amendment, Americans are protected against "unreasonable searches and seizures," meaning the government cannot enter a person's home to seek evidence without a search warrant. The Fourth Amendment guarantees that a court maintains overview of criminal investigations involving such searches.

The Fifth Amendment provides other important legal safeguards. It guarantees "due process of law," meaning the courts must treat all defendants equally, and grants protection against self-incrimination, shielding Americans from testifying against their better interests or otherwise involuntarily providing evidence to prosecutors.

The Sixth Amendment guarantees the right to a "speedy and public trial." In other words, the government is prohibited from arresting a defendant and throwing him or her into jail for years, then convening a trial in a courtroom closed to public scrutiny. The amendment traces its roots to the Court of Star Chamber, a seventeenth-century courtroom in England in which secret trials were held against subjects who had crossed the king. Star Chamber defendants were invariably convicted on the strength of farcical evidence, the phoniness of which never came to light because the trials were held in secret.

The Seventh Amendment guarantees the right to a trial by jury, while the Eighth Amendment guards against "cruel and unusual punishment." For a society that had, in years past, approved of witch burnings, the Eighth Amendment provided an important protection to criminal defendants.

The Road to Ratification Continues

The final two amendments reflect an effort by Congress to allay the concerns of the Anti-Federalists, who feared—even with the inclusion of the

The original Bill of Rights, as it appeared after being presented to and passed by the US Senate in 1789, is shown in this photograph. After full Congressional debate and revision, the first ten amendments to the Constitution became law in 1791.

The Conventions of a Number of the States having, at the Time of their adopting the Constitution, expressed a Desire, in Order to prevent misconstruction or abuse of its Powers, that further declaratory and restrictive Clauses should be added: And as extending the Ground of public Confidence in the Government, will best insure the beneficent ends of its Institution—

RESOLVED, BY THE SENATE AND HOUSE OF REPRESENTATIVES OF THE UNITED STATES OF AMERICA IN CONGRESS ASSEMBLED, two thirds of both Houses concurring, That the following articles be proposed to the Legislatures of the several States, as amendments to the Constitution of the United States, all or any of which articles, when ratified by three fourths of the said Legislatures, to be valid to all intents and purposes, as part of the said Constitution—Viz.

ARTICLES in addition to, and amendment of, the Constitution of the United States of America, proposed by Congress, and ratified by the Legislatures of the several States, pursuant to the fifth Article of the original Constitution.

ARTICLE the FIRST.

After the first enumeration, required by the first article of the Constitution, there shall be one Representative for every thirty thousand, until the number shall amount to one hundred; to which number one Representative shall be added for every subsequent increase of forty thousand, until the Representatives shall amount to two hundred, to wh   r one Representative shall be added f   ty thou
perso

ARTICLE the SECOND.

No law, varying the compensation for the services of the Senators and Representatives, shall take effect, until an election of Representatives shall have intervened.

ARTICLE the THIRD.

Congress shall make no law establishing articles of faith, or a mode of worship, or prohibiting the free exercise of religion, or abridging the freedom of speech, or of the press, or the right of the people peaceably to assemble, and to petition to the government for a redress of grievances.

ARTICLE the FOURTH.

A well regulated militia, being necessary to the security of a free State, the right of the people to keep and bear arms, shall not be infringed.

ARTICLE the FIFTH.

No soldier shall, in time of peace, be quartered in any house, without the consent of the owner, nor in time of war, but in a manner to be prescribed by law.

ARTICLE the SIXTH.

The right of the people to be secure in their persons, houses, papers, and effects, against unreasonable searches and seizures, shall not be violated, and no warrants shall issue, but upon probable cause, supported by oath or affirmation, and particularly describing the place to be searched, and the persons or things to be seized.

The Whiskey Rebellion

It did not take long for the powers of the Constitution to be called into use to protect the country from a crisis. In 1791, to help repay the national debt, Congress adopted a tax on whiskey sales in America. The tax was met with hostility in western Pennsylvania, where many farmers distilled and sold corn whiskey. In 1794 a group of angry farmers destroyed the home of a federal tax official. Others learned of the mischief and joined the cause.

News of the rebellion reached George Washington, who feared the eruption of a widespread insurrection similar to Shays's Rebellion. Washington at first hoped to negotiate with the rebels, but when attempts at diplomacy failed, he called up state militias and sent thirteen thousand troops to western Pennsylvania.

In the face of such an overwhelming force, the rebellion was quick to collapse. Two of the rebel leaders were convicted of treason, but Washington granted them pardons. Washington's quick response to the rebellion proved the federal government had the will, and the constitutionally mandated authority, to respond to a national crisis.

Bill of Rights—that the Constitution would endow the federal government with excessive authority. The Ninth Amendment essentially says the first eight amendments are not intended to cover all rights guaranteed to Americans, and the fact that those unnamed rights have not been included does not mean they do not exist. As such, the Ninth Amendment states, those rights—whatever they may be—are still guaranteed to the people. And the Tenth Amendment guarantees that the powers which have not been delegated to the federal government can be assumed by the state governments, or by the people of the United States.

In 1791, after the constitutionally required three-fourths of the states adopted the amendments, these rights assumed the force of law the Anti-Federalists demanded. Ratification was not yet complete, however. Four years after adoption of the Bill of Rights, the Eleventh Amendment was ratified. It was a victory for states' rights advocates, providing states a measure of legal protection by shielding them from lawsuits filed in federal courts. In fact, since the Constitution was ratified, the document has been amended twenty-seven times: proof that the formation of a more perfect union did not end in 1788 but is, rather, an ongoing and evolving process.

What Is the Legacy of the Constitution and Its Role in the Founding of a New Nation?

During the War of Independence, the Continental Congress found a devoted ally in France. Great Britain's longtime enemy had its own reasons for helping the Americans—the French and Indian War as well as a series of defeats in European wars had weakened the French, costing them valuable colonies in Canada as well as the Near East. By helping the Americans, the French hoped to undermine the British and recover some of their lost colonies. In addition to making loans to the Continental Congress, the French lent one of their best generals, the Marquis de La Fayette, to the Continental army. La Fayette's leadership was instrumental at Yorktown, helping George Washington defeat Cornwallis.

It can be said the French learned a lot from the American Revolution and the Constitutional Convention, because in 1789 the people of France rose up against their monarch, Louis XVI. The French National Assembly was convened and soon adopted the Declaration of the Rights of Man and of the Citizen. The declaration, which served as a preamble to the new French constitution, is similar to the American

Bill of Rights in that it guarantees freedom of speech and of the press, religious tolerance, and equal justice under the law. Perhaps the most radical pronouncement in the declaration was its refusal to observe the "divine right" of kings to rule. This right—in which monarchs claim their authority to govern is endowed by God—had been a guiding force in the history of France since medieval times. Now, the French people declared, they would govern themselves.

The new constitution did permit Louis to remain on the throne, however, ruling as a "constitutional monarch." Under this form of government, many of the king's powers were assumed by the National Assembly. Louis bristled under these reins placed on his authority; meanwhile, many people in France believed that for their country to be a true republic, no king should remain in power. Finally, in 1792 the republicans prevailed and overthrew the king—Louis was dispatched on the guillotine in 1793—and the First French Republic was established.

Reign of Terror

While it seemed as though the French had achieved a measure of popular rule comparable to the democracy enjoyed in America, this was not the case. In America the Anti-Federalists may have worried about the creation of an oligarchy, but the checks and balances written into the US Constitution prevented the concentration of power into the hands of a few.

The new French constitution, however, lacked sufficient checks and balances, and soon a powerful elite emerged within the National Assembly, known as the Committee of Public Safety. Led by an elected member of the assembly, Maximilien de Robespierre, the Committee of Public Safety governed as an oligarchy. It ruled during a dark period of French history known as the Reign of Terror, in which thousands of the committee's perceived enemies were rounded up, imprisoned, and executed. Robespierre and his allies were overthrown in 1794, but the unrest continued until 1799 when a young military officer, Napoleón Bonaparte, seized power, eventually assuming dictatorial powers and declaring himself emperor.

France's failed experiment in self-governance illustrates how the weakness of the French constitution led to widespread chaos, political upheaval, and the rule of a dictator. France eventually achieved lasting democracy in 1870 with the establishment of the Third Republic. Other countries were much slower to turn away from their monarchs. Following the catastrophe of World War I—a war sparked by the jealousies and lust for power harbored by a handful of European monarchs—many European countries moved to dethrone their kings and adopt republican forms of government based on the American model of democracy.

Many of these attempts fell short. In places such as Russia, Germany, Italy, and Spain, weak constitutions failed to provide reformers with strong foundations on which to rebuild their war-torn societies. In Russia, for example, after the monarchy collapsed in 1917, a democratic gov-

The execution of Louis XVI, king of France, in 1793 (pictured) ushered in the First French Republic. The leaders of the French uprising adopted a declaration of rights that had similarities to the US Bill of Rights, but France's early efforts at self-governance failed miserably.

ernment lasted less than eight months before it was unseated by a Communist oligarchy that endured into the 1990s. And the fascist regimes that seized power in Germany and Italy caused much suffering throughout the European continent and ultimately sparked World War II.

The Flawed German Constitution

Indeed, following World War I the Germans ousted their monarch and made a good faith effort to establish an effective constitution to govern their new republic. The German constitution, adopted in 1919, included phrases such as "political power emanates from the people" and "all Germans are equal before the law."[52] The German constitution also guaranteed freedom of assembly, speech, and equal justice.

But the German constitution was flawed. It endowed the chief executive—the chancellor—with dictatorial powers during national emergencies. After Adolf Hitler assumed the chancellorship of Germany in 1933, he used this provision to seize control and plunge the European continent into war. Says journalist William L. Shirer, who covered the rise of Hitler, "There were flaws [in the constitution] to be sure, and in the end some of them proved disastrous."[53]

After World War II, many countries in Europe and other corners of the world based their constitutions on the American model, and these bodies of law have endured into the twenty-first century. Says former Rutgers University Law School professor Albert P. Blaustein, "The US Constitution is America's most important export."[54]

A Warning from Washington

Unlike the failed attempts to establish republican governments in places like France, Russia, and Germany, American democracy has remained intact—despite some obvious flaws in the US Constitution. Indeed, George Washington was among the first of the national leaders to recognize that the Constitution failed to rein in certain abuses he feared would plague the government for decades to come.

As Washington prepared to leave the presidency near the end of two terms in office, he issued a warning to the American people: He admonished them to be wary of political parties, for he believed such parties are more likely to work for the benefit of influential minorities than toward goals intended to aid all people. In his farewell address, first published in 1796, Washington said:

> The common and continual mischiefs of the spirit of party are sufficient to make it the interest and duty of a wise people to discourage and restrain it. It serves always to distract the public councils and enfeeble the public administration. It agitates the community with ill-founded jealousies and false alarms, kindles the animosity of one part against another [leading to] occasionally riot and insurrection. It opens the door to foreign influence and corruption, which finds a facilitated access to the government itself through the channels of party passions.[55]

Washington was not the only Founding Father to be concerned about the influence of political parties on American society and politics. In the Federalist Papers, James Madison and Alexander Hamilton both wrote about their fears that parties—which they often referred to as "factions"—would seek legislation that would benefit the individuals and groups who pulled their strings. Nevertheless, Madison and Hamilton also believed the Constitution contains sufficient safeguards that ensure Congress could do its job free of the pressures political parties bring to bear.

In Federalist No. 10, for example, Madison said article 1 of the Constitution, which provides for the direct election of members of Congress by the people, serves as a restraint on the influence of political parties. He argued citizens would be able to see through the lies and true intentions of party leaders as well as influential insiders who dictate the policies party leaders follow, and instead cast their ballots for honest and well-intentioned candidates. Madison predicted:

As each representative will be chosen by a greater number of citizens . . . it will be more difficult for unworthy candidates to practice with success the vicious arts by which elections are too often carried; and the suffrages of the people being more free, will be more likely to centre in men who possess the most attractive merit and the most diffusive and established characters.[56]

The Constitution includes no further language to limit the influence of parties, other than providing a framework under which federal officials are elected, because the authors of the Constitution believed the union and political system they were creating would be strong enough to withstand the influences of political organizations.

The Lobbying Industry

Clearly, Madison, Hamilton, and the other authors of the Constitution got it wrong. Today every institution created by the Constitution—the presidency, Congress, and even the Supreme Court—reflect the influences of the modern Democratic and Republican Parties. In fact, all members of Congress owe their seats to the work done on their behalf by the political parties—even those elected as independents can usually count on support from one of the parties.

If Hamilton and Madison were alive today to see how the parties have taken control of Washington, DC, they would realize that not only did the Constitution contain no language that would restrict the influence of the parties, it actually includes language that has encouraged the growth of factions.

The First Amendment guarantees the right of the people to "petition the Government for a redress of grievances." Those eight words have led to the growth of the lobbying community, whose participants are professionals paid by special-interest groups. Lobbyists often represent business-related organizations and labor unions as well as a myriad of others—such as gun owners, abortion opponents, gay rights activists, and environmentalists—to pressure members of Congress to adopt legislation that would benefit their clients. The term *lobbyist* dates back to 1830s London, when

Gerrymandering

The US Constitution addresses representation in Congress in article 1 as well as in the Fourteenth Amendment. Under the terms of the Constitution, US House districts are to be reapportioned every ten years following completion of the US Census. In other words, the 435 House district boundaries are realigned to reflect the shifts in population that occurred in the previous decade.

However, the political parties often use their influence to carve out "safe" districts for their incumbents, ensuring that concentrations of voters who belong to opposing parties are shifted into neighboring districts. This process is known as "gerrymandering" and is named after Elbridge Gerry, a delegate to the 1787 Constitutional Convention, who was the first political leader to draw legislative borders to benefit specific candidates.

The result of gerrymandering means that fewer and fewer congressional districts are competitive. According to political analyst Nate Silver, in 1992, 103 congressional districts were considered "swing" districts, meaning either party had a fair chance to win the districts in an election. By 2012 Silver estimated that just 35 congressional districts remained competitive.

Under the terms of the US Constitution, voters are supposed to select their representatives, but some political analysts believe the opposite is now true. Says a statement by the watchdog group Center for Voting and Democracy, "By gerrymandering the districts, legislators and their political cronies have used redistricting to choose their voters, before voters have had the opportunity to choose them."

Center for Voting and Democracy, "Redistricting," 2012. www.fairvote.org.

much of the wheeling and dealing on new laws was conducted in the lob-by outside the parliamentary chamber; some four decades later President Ulysses S. Grant is said to have often left the White House for a stroll to the nearby Willard Hotel, where he would take a seat in the lobby to enjoy a cigar and brandy. Political party leaders and other influential citizens knew Grant's schedule and often descended on the Willard lobby to hand him letters and petitions demanding adoption of new laws.

In 2012 James Thurber, a political science professor at American University, published a report on the influence of lobbyists on Ameri-can politics—particularly on Congress. Thurber estimates that more than one hundred thousand professionals are employed in what has become the American lobbying industry, and each year lobbies spend more than $9 billion—mostly in contributions to political parties and campaign organizations for incumbents and candidates—to influence their votes on bills. "The Catholic Church has lobbyists," says Thurber. "The Boy Scouts have lobbyists. The AFL-CIO [a labor union] has lob-byists. Apple does. Everybody has a lobbyist."[57]

With such vast sums of money spent to influence legislation, it is clear that the factions Washington warned about—and that Madison and Hamilton felt confident could never have a significant influence on the federal government—have become very much a factor in the way politicians in Washington, DC, operate. Says Thurber:

> I think that when people give campaign contributions, they are not there simply to improve the workings of democracy. They're there to buy access. . . . Everybody in Washington who's a lobbyist gives campaign contributions. . . . The iron law of reciprocity—meaning, "I'll help you if you'll help me"—is ingrained in politics. It's ingrained on [Capitol] Hill. . . . That's perfectly legal.[58]

The Abolition of Slavery

Although lobbying in America has been around at least since Grant's day, the power of the lobbying community did not truly explode until the twentieth century. In the 1930s the federal government started spending vast sums of money to implement the New Deal programs to rescue the country from the Great Depression. As part of the New Deal, Congress authorized huge public works projects such as the construction of dams and roads and the electrification of rural areas. Later in the decade Congress invested heavily in the military as World War II grew more imminent. As businesses vied for huge government contracts, they sent lobbyists to Washington to press their cases. Lobbying continues to influence the lawmaking process, but Congress has taken some steps to limit this influence, such as making lobbyists register and thereby publicly identify themselves.

Other deficiencies in the Constitution surfaced much earlier and required much more than just legislative corrections. Indeed, the failure of the Constitution to address the morality of slavery led to dire consequences that tested the strength of the union.

As the delegates left Philadelphia in 1787 to return to their home states, many who opposed slavery were dissatisfied that the Constitution failed to address the status of the slaves, other than to determine how they would be counted for electoral purposes. Some delegates committed their lives to the abolition of slavery. Among them was Benjamin Franklin, who had once owned slaves but freed them, finding he could not in good conscience own other human beings. Franklin's newspaper, the *Pennsylvania Gazette*, also stopped accepting advertisements from people who desired to sell their slaves. In 1787, the same year he signed the Constitution that gave the weight of law to the Three-Fifths Compromise, Franklin ascended to the presidency of the nation's first abolitionist group, the Society for Promoting the Abolition of Slavery and the Relief of Negroes Unlawfully Held in Bondage. In February 1790 Franklin sought a redress of grievances by delivering a petition to Congress that called for the emancipation of the slaves. In it he declared, "Mankind are all formed by the same Almighty Being, alike the objects of his care, and equally designed for the enjoyment of happiness."[59]

Dred Scott and the Civil War

The petition failed to find support in Congress, and Franklin died just two months later. Other abolitionists, however, took up the cause, and eventually the issue divided the nation as northern abolitionists continued to campaign for emancipation while southerners, whose politics were dictated by wealthy plantation owners, insisted on keeping slavery as an institution.

The Supreme Court—a creation of article 3—weighed in on the issue in 1857 after the slave Dred Scott sued his owner, contending slavery to be unconstitutional. In the *Scott* case the court ruled that since Scott was a citizen of Africa and not the United States, he had no standing to challenge an American law. And so the court found no constitutional grounds on which to ban slavery.

Union and Confederate soldiers wage war during the Battle of Bull Run in 1861. Hostility toward a compromise over slavery during the Constitutional Convention festered, eventually driving a ruinous wedge between the states. The resulting Civil War led to hundreds of thousands of American deaths.

The *Scott* decision was written by Roger B. Taney, chief justice of the United States, who exemplified the partisanship Washington had warned about. He was an ally of former president Andrew Jackson, who devised the "spoils" system that rewards friends and supporters with political jobs. Jackson forged the modern Democratic Party and helped make it the most powerful political organization in America in the pre–Civil War years. Before Jackson appointed him to the Supreme Court, Taney served as Jackson's attorney general, using the authority of the federal government to ensure slavery remained a part of American society.

Despite the *Scott* decision, the campaign for abolition continued to gain fervor in the North while the South continued to resist. Finally, in 1861 the Civil War erupted as the southern states seceded from the union.

Separate but Equal

After the Civil War, slavery was outlawed with adoption of the Thirteenth Amendment, while the Fourteenth Amendment granted citizenship to the emancipated slaves, thereby repealing the Three-Fifths Compromise. The Fifteenth Amendment provided male citizens of all races the right to vote. (However, it took until 1920, and the adoption of the Nineteenth Amendment, for women of all races to be granted suffrage.)

The slaves had been freed by a bloody civil war that cost the lives of more than six hundred thousand Americans, but as the southern states rejoined the union, they were slow to grant rights to their new citizens. Prejudice remained a part of American life for decades. In the southern states, "whites-only" restaurants, theaters, public restrooms, railroad cars, and schools were established. Here, again, the Supreme Court showed how partisanship could flavor its decisions when it ruled in the 1896 *Plessy v. Ferguson* case that institutions in American society could separate train passengers, theatergoers, students, and others by race as long as the people of the various races were provided an equal quality of services. The *Plessy* decision established the precedent that a "separate but equal" standard is constitutionally acceptable.

Winning the Vote but Losing the Election

Under the terms of the US Constitution, the candidate for president who wins the most popular votes is not necessarily declared the winner. In fact, such a circumstance has occurred four times in the nation's history—in 1824, 1876, 1888, and 2000.

In the 2000 presidential election, Democrat Al Gore, the vice president, received some five hundred thousand more votes than his opponent, Republican George W. Bush. And yet Bush was declared the winner of the election.

Bush won because he received more votes in the Electoral College, an institution established in article 2 of the Constitution. The states send members to the Electoral College based on the number of representatives and senators they send to Congress. Following the presidential election, the Electoral College members cast votes for the candidates who win the popular votes in their states. Most state delegations cast "winner take all" votes, meaning large states like California or New York cast all their Electoral College votes for the winners of their popular votes. But if a candidate wins large blocs of states with much smaller populations, that candidate can remain competitive in the Electoral College even though the candidate's popular vote counts are relatively small.

This is what happened in 2000. In the election, Gore won just twenty states, as well as the District of Columbia, receiving 266 votes in the Electoral College. Bush won thirty states, and the presidency, with 271 Electoral College votes, even though he trailed Gore in the overall popular vote.

The court's decision was written by Justice Henry Billings Brown, a well-known social Darwinist—meaning he believed that evolution favored some racial and ethnic groups over others. Social Darwinism is a racist theory and is reflected in Brown's decision. In his opinion, he declared that separate but equal did not violate the Fourteenth Amendment, which guarantees equal protection under the law. The separate but equal standard, found to be constitutional by the nation's highest court, remained law in America until the Supreme Court's *Brown v. Board of Education* decision of 1954 overturned the standard and ordered the desegregation of all schools and other institutions of American life.

Power of the Supreme Court

The *Plessy v. Ferguson* and *Brown v. Board of Education* decisions illustrate how the Supreme Court applies its constitutionally mandated power as interpreter of the Constitution and how the court's interpretations can evolve as society changes. Indeed, in recent years the Supreme Court has been asked to apply interpretations of the Constitution to a variety of issues that did not exist during the era in which the document was debated.

The court's decision in the case challenging the Affordable Care Act serves as one example. Another clear example can be found in the 1973 *Roe v. Wade* decision, which declared abortion legal under the terms of the Fourteenth Amendment to the Constitution, which guarantees that no state government has the right to deprive citizens of "life, liberty or property." Courts have interpreted this clause to mean that states shall not pry into the private affairs of a citizen— such as a woman's decision to seek an abortion. In the years since *Roe v. Wade*, many antiabortion groups have challenged the law, and some cases have made it as far as the Supreme Court, but by 2013 the *Roe v. Wade* decision remained the guiding force on abortion law in America.

Gay rights and, specifically, the question of whether the Fourteenth Amendment guarantee of equal protection can be used to negate state laws barring marriage between gays is another contemporary issue that has undergone scrutiny by the Supreme Court. And in 2013, in the wake of a rash of incidents involving gun violence—including the murders of twenty first-graders and six adults at a Connecticut elementary

At a gun rights rally in Louisiana in 2013 a protester displays the Second Amendment. The Constitution and Bill of Rights have guided American life for more than 220 years. Despite sometimes impassioned debate, they will continue to do so for years to come.

school in 2012—lawmakers in Washington planned to introduce new measures to control gun ownership. Gun rights activists, including the National Rifle Association—a lobbying organization—are certain to challenge the constitutionality of the measures, contending they violate Second Amendment rights.

The American Republic Endures

The partisanship that worried the Founding Fathers is very much a fact of life in Washington in the twenty-first century. Congress is gridlocked on many issues as the parties, often controlled by their extremist elements, refuse to compromise. Indeed, in the 2010 *Citizens United v. Federal Election Commission* case, the Supreme Court threw out a federal law limiting the amount of money corporations, labor unions, and other institutions could contribute in support of political causes. In making its finding, the Supreme Court extended the First Amendment right of free speech to such groups.

Loyola University law school professor Jessica Levinson says big spenders have used the power granted to them by the Supreme Court to mute the voices of ordinary people. "In its effort to protect speech rights, the court has trampled on them," she says. "By giving spenders as much speech as they can buy, we leave listeners in a political marketplace flooded by high-spending speakers who drown out the rest of us."[60] Adds *Buffalo News* columnist Douglas Turner, "Big money protects the incumbency and encourages gridlock. It isolates Congress from the average voter."[61]

But partisanship, legislative gridlock, and the influence of lobbyists and other legacies of the Constitution are the prices Americans have learned to pay for the Constitution's far more desirable legacies: the rights and freedoms that have endured in their country since ratification in 1788. Unlike the failed democracies of France, Germany, and Russia, the American republic has remained strong—even withstanding a devastating civil war—in no small part due to the resiliency of the US Constitution and the role it played in the founding of the nation.

Source Notes

Introduction: What Are the Defining Characteristics of the US Constitution?

1. Quoted in Bill Mears and Tom Cohen, "Emotions High After Supreme Court Upholds Health Care Law," CNN, June 28, 2012. www.cnn.com.
2. David A. Strauss, *The Living Constitution*. New York: Oxford University Press, 2010, pp. 1–2.
3. Quoted in Johnson County (Kansas) Republican Party, "Affordable Care Act Is Unconstitutional," Facebook, August 12, 2011. www.facebook.com.
4. Quoted in Mears and Cohen, "Emotions High After Supreme Court Upholds Health Care Law."
5. Richard Beeman, *Plain, Honest Men: The Making of the American Constitution*. New York: Random House, 2009, pp. xiii–xiv.

Chapter One: What Conditions Led to the Need for the Constitution and the Founding of a New Nation?

6. Quoted in William H. Whitmore, ed., *The Colonial Laws of Massachusetts*. Boston: Rockwell & Churchill, 1890, p. 33.
7. Quoted in Whitmore, *The Colonial Laws of Massachusetts*, p. 55.
8. Quoted in A.J. Langguth, *Patriots: The Men Who Started the American Revolution*. New York: Simon & Schuster, 1988, p. 49.
9. Quoted in Dennis B. Fraden, *Samuel Adams: The Father of American Independence*. New York: Clarion, 1998, p. 26.
10. Quoted in Akhil Reed Amar, *America's Constitution: A Biography*. New York: Random House, 2005, p. 105.
11. Quoted in National Park Service, "Martial Law at Jamestown," October 18, 2012. www.nps.gov.
12. Quoted in Nathaniel Philbrick, *Mayflower: A Story of Courage, Community, and War*. New York: Penguin, 2007, p. 41.

13. Quoted in New York Historical Society, "Alexander Hamilton: The Man Who Made Modern America," 2004. www.alexanderhamilton exhibition.org.

Chapter Two: Crises in the New Nation

14. Quoted in Yale School of Law, "Articles of Confederation," 2008. http://avalon.law.yale.edu.

15. Mark Roe, "America's First Debt Crisis," Project Syndicate, August 8, 2011. www.project-syndicate.org.

16. Quoted in Catherine Drinker Bowen, *Miracle in Philadelphia: The Story of the Constitutional Convention, May to September 1787.* Boston: Little, Brown, 1986, p. 7.

17. Quoted in Beeman, *Plain, Honest Men*, p. 377.

18. Quoted in Ron Michener, "Money in the American Colonies," Economic History Association, February 1, 2010. http://eh.net.

19. Larry Allen, *The Encyclopedia of Money*. Santa Barbara, CA: ABC-CLIO, 2009, p. 200.

20. Quoted in David P. Szatmary, *Shays' Rebellion: The Making of an Agrarian Insurrection*. Amherst: University of Massachusetts Press, 1980, p. 72.

21. Quoted in Szatmary, *Shays' Rebellion*, p. 73.

22. Quoted in Beeman, *Plain, Honest Men*, p. 17.

23. Quoted in Ron Chernow, *Alexander Hamilton*. New York: Penguin, 2005, p. 225.

24. Beeman, *Plain, Honest Men*, p. 19.

25. Quoted in Beeman, *Plain, Honest Men*, p. 19.

26. Quoted in Beeman, *Plain, Honest Men*, p. 20.

Chapter Three: A Summer in Philadelphia

27. Quoted in Bowen, *Miracle in Philadelphia*, p. 13.

28. Quoted in Kevin R.C. Gutzman, *James Madison and the Making of America*. New York: St. Martin's, 2012, p. 67.

29. Quoted in Beeman, *Plain, Honest Men*, p. 88.

30. Quoted in Bowen, *Miracle in Philadelphia*, p. 107.

31. Quoted in Beeman, *Plain, Honest Men*, p. 89.

32. Quoted in Thomas Fleming, *The Making of the Constitution*. Boston: New World City, 2011. Kindle edition.

33. Quoted in Walter Isaacson, *Benjamin Franklin: An American Life*. New York: Simon & Schuster, 2003, p. 449.

34. Isaacson, *Benjamin Franklin*, p. 453.

35. Quoted in Beeman, *Plain, Honest Men*, p. 319.

36. Quoted in Bowen, *Miracle in Philadelphia*, p. 202.

37. Quoted in Bowen, *Miracle in Philadelphia*, p. 201.

38. Quoted in Beeman, *Plain, Honest Men*, p. 319.

39. Bowen, *Miracle in Philadelphia*, p. 201.

40. Quoted in Beeman, *Plain, Honest Men*, p. 138.

Chapter Four: The Road to Ratification

41. Quoted in Herbert J. Storing, ed., *The Complete Anti-Federalist*. Chicago: University of Chicago Press, 1981, p. 114.

42. Jack N. Rakove, *Original Meanings: Politics and Ideas in the Making of the Constitution*. New York: Vintage, 1997, pp. 324–325.

43. Quoted in Storing, *The Complete Anti-Federalist*, p. 114.

44. Quoted in Anthony R. Fellow, *American Media History*. Boston: Wadsworth, 2010, p. 31.

45. Quoted in Fellow, *American Media History*, p. 32.

46. Quoted in Fellow, *American Media History*, p. 33.

47. Quoted in Beeman, *Plain, Honest Men*, p. 398.

48. Quoted in Bowen, *Miracle in Philadelphia*, p. 270.

49. Federalist No. 1, introduction, Constitution Society, November 11, 2011. www.constitution.org.

50. Federalist No. 2, "Concerning Dangers from Foreign Force and Influence," Constitution Society, November 11, 2011. www.constitution.org.

51. Federalist No. 9, "The Utility of the Union as a Safeguard Against Domestic Faction and Insurrection," Constitution Society, November 11, 2011. www.constitution.org.

Chapter Five: What Is the Legacy of the Constitution and Its Role in the Founding of a New Nation?

52. Quoted in William L. Shirer, *The Rise and Fall of the Third Reich: A History of Nazi Germany*. New York: Simon & Schuster, 1960, p. 57.

53. Shirer, *The Rise and Fall of the Third Reich*, p. 56.

54. Albert P. Blaustein, "Our Most Important Export: The Influence of the United States Constitution Abroad," *Connecticut Journal of International Law*, 1987–1988, p. 15.

55. Quoted in Dennis Jamison, "George Washington's Views on Political Parties in America," *Washington Times*, March 9, 2012. http://communities.washingtontimes.com.

56. Federalist No. 10, "The Utility of the Union as a Safeguard Against Domestic Faction and Insurrection," Constitution Society, November 11, 2011. www.constitution.org.

57. Quoted in Sharyl Attkisson, "Behind the Closed Doors of Washington Lobbyists," CBS News, October 7, 2012. www.cbsnews.com.

58. Quoted in Attkisson, "Behind the Closed Doors of Washington Lobbyists."

59. Quoted in Franklin Wood, *The Americanization of Benjamin Franklin*. New York: Penguin, 2004, p. 228.

60. Jessica Levinson, "Citizens United Gives Free Speech a High Price," Politico, June 20, 2012. www.politico.com.

61. Douglas Turner, "River of Cash Impedes Fight Against Citizens United," *Buffalo (NY) News*, December 10, 2012. www.buffalonews.com.

Important People in the History of the Constitution and the Founding of a New Nation

Benjamin Franklin: A printer, inventor, diplomat, and statesman, Franklin signed the Declaration of Independence then represented Pennsylvania at the Constitutional Convention. Along with John Dickinson of Delaware and Roger Sherman of Connecticut, Franklin helped broker the Great Compromise, which determined how the states would be represented in Congress.

Elbridge Gerry: Although he was a signer of the Declaration of Independence, an author of the Articles of Confederation, and a delegate representing Massachusetts at the Constitutional Convention, Gerry is best known as the first practitioner of gerrymandering, in which the boundaries of legislative districts are redrawn to favor specific candidates and their parties.

Alexander Hamilton: An early and enthusiastic supporter of the Constitutional Convention, Hamilton played an influential role at the Philadelphia convention in helping craft the system of government that prevailed in the debate. Following the convention, Hamilton was one of three authors of the Federalist Papers and went on to serve as the first secretary of the treasury.

John Jay: Following the Constitutional Convention the delegate from New York State was one of three authors of the Federalist Papers. After ratification Jay served as a diplomat in Great Britain and was later appointed the first chief justice of the United States, presiding over the Supreme Court. His political career also included service as governor of New York.

James Madison: A plantation owner from Virginia, Madison was the author of the Virginia Plan, the original blueprint for the US Constitution, which established three coequal branches of government: legislative, executive, and judicial. Following the convention, Madison helped author the Federalist Papers and later served as fourth president of the United States.

Luther Martin: The delegate from Maryland was a vehement opponent of slavery and derided his fellow delegates for not regarding slavery as a moral wrong that should be outlawed in the Constitution. At the conclusion of the convention, he refused to place his signature on the new body of laws.

Gouverneur Morris: The delegate from Pennsylvania served on the Constitutional Convention's Committee of Style and Arrangement, charged with rendering the Constitution into written form. Morris is the author of the Constitution's Preamble, which lays out the goals of the Constitution by opening with the words: "We the people of the United States, in Order to form a more perfect Union."

William Paterson: The delegate from New Jersey opposed the Virginia Plan because he believed it endowed the federal government with too much authority over the states. Paterson proposed an alternate plan, titled the New Jersey Plan, that limited each state's representation in Congress to one member.

Edmund Randolph: The governor of Virginia headed his delegation to the Constitutional Convention in Philadelphia and opened the debate on May 29, 1787, by proposing the Virginia Plan. Following ratification, Randolph went on to serve as secretary of state and then attorney general.

Daniel Shays: The farmer from Massachusetts led the insurrection against court-ordered seizures of farmers' lands in the years following the War of Independence. Shays's Rebellion helped convince wary political leaders of the need for a strong central government. The rebellion was eventually put down and Shays convicted of treason, although he was later pardoned.

Roger B. Taney: A chief justice of the United States appointed by President Andrew Jackson, Taney exemplified the partisanship about which George Washington had warned as he prepared to leave office. In 1857 Taney found constitutional grounds to protect slavery when he ruled in the *Dred Scott* case.

George Washington: The Virginia plantation owner led the Continental army during the War of Independence, eventually defeating British general Lord Charles Cornwallis at Yorktown to secure victory for the United States. Washington presided over the Constitutional Convention and was elected the first president under the terms of the Constitution.

Thomas West: The governor of Jamestown arrived in the beleaguered colony in 1610, determined to save it from starvation and infighting. To establish order, West, along with colonists Thomas Gates and Thomas Dale, authored thirty-seven statutes to govern the colony. The document, spanning eighteen handwritten pages, is known as the Laws Divine, Moral and Martial.

James Wilson: A delegate from Pennsylvania, Wilson was a major advocate for checks and balances to ensure all three branches of government remain coequal. Wilson insisted Congress be granted authority to override presidential vetoes. He was also an advocate for the Necessary and Proper Clause, which provides the federal government with general authority rather than specific duties.

John Peter Zenger: In 1733 the publisher from New York enraged the royal governor, William Cosby, by publishing stories alleging misconduct. Cosby had Zenger arrested and charged with libel, but Zenger's attorney, Andrew Hamilton, convinced a jury that Zenger was innocent because he printed the truth. Zenger's case established the principle of freedom of the press in America.

For Further Research

Books

Faculty of Hillsdale College, *The US Constitution: A Reader*. Hillsdale, MI: Hillsdale College, 2012.

Kevin R.C. Gutzman, *James Madison and the Making of America*. New York: St. Martin's, 2012.

Pauline Maier, *Ratification: The People Debate the Constitution, 1787–1788*. New York: Simon & Schuster, 2011.

Brion McClanahan, *The Founding Fathers' Guide to the Constitution*. Washington, DC: Regnery History, 2012.

William Nester, *The Hamiltonian Vision, 1789–1800: The Art of American Power During the Early Republic*. Dulles, VA: Potomac, 2012.

Anthony J. Nownes, *Interest Groups in American Politics: Pressure and Power*. New York: Routledge, 2013.

William Bennett Turner, *Figures of Speech: First Amendment Heroes and Villains*. San Francisco: Berrett-Koehler, 2011.

George William Van Cleve, *A Slaveholders' Union: Slavery, Politics, and the Constitution in the Early American Republic*. Chicago: University of Chicago Press, 2011.

Websites

Articles of Confederation (www.loc.gov/rr/program/bib/ourdocs/articles.html). Maintained by the US Library of Congress, the site provides a text of the Articles of Confederation as well as images of early printed copies of the document that served as the nation's first set of laws. The

Library of Congress provides a search engine to enable visitors to find specific provisions covered in the Articles.

Constitution of the United States (www.archives.gov/exhibits/char ters/constitution.html). The National Archives and Records Administration serves as custodian of the original copy of the US Constitution. Visitors to the National Archives website can find images of the original handwritten pages composed during the convention of 1787, a complete transcript of the document, and a history of the events surrounding the debate over the Constitution.

Federalist Papers (http://thomas.loc.gov/home/histdox/fedpapers .html). The Library of Congress maintains a complete archive of all eighty-five Federalist Papers, the newspaper essays written by James Madison, Alexander Hamilton, and John Jay to counter Anti-Federalist arguments against ratification. Students can download the text of each essay.

First Amendment Center (www.firstamendmentcenter.org). Sponsored by Vanderbilt University and the Newseum, the museum devoted to the American press, the center's website provides many resources on the First Amendment. By following the link for the "State of the First Amendment," students can read essays by constitutional scholars on efforts in US history to strengthen or undermine First Amendment rights.

Martial Law at Jamestown (www.nps.gov/jame/historyculture/martial -law.htm). The National Park Service maintains this website to chronicle the early laws that governed the Jamestown colony in Virginia. Students can find excerpts from the Laws Divine, Moral and Martial written in 1610 by governor Thomas West, as well as other leaders of the colony, to restore order to Jamestown after attempts to live under British law failed.

National Constitution Center (http://constitutioncenter.org). Located in Philadelphia, the National Constitution Center includes many exhibits celebrating the history of the Constitution and its impacts on American life. By following the link for the "Interactive Constitution," visitors can use a search engine to find specific provisions of the Constitution and how they affect a variety of issues from abortion to taxes.

Twelve Tables (www.csun.edu/~hcfll004/12tables.html). Sponsored by California State University–Northridge, the site includes the text of the Twelve Tables, the original written laws that guided the Roman republic. The first laws written with the participation of the people they would govern covered topics such as the procedures for the conduct of trials, the repaying of debts, and the rights of landowners.

US Debt and Foreign Loans, 1775–1795 (http://history.state.gov/milestones/1784-1800/Loans). The site maintained by the US Department of State chronicles the enormous foreign debt that saddled the new US government following the War of Independence. The site describes the financial help the French provided, as well as the limited authority granted to the Continental Congress under the Articles of Confederation to repay foreign debts at the conclusion of the war.

Index

Note: Boldface page numbers indicate illustrations.

abolition, 45, 74–76
abortion, 78
Adams, Samuel, 16
Allen, Larry, 29, 30
Ames, Fisher, 32
Annapolis Convention, 35, 36
Annapolis Report, 36
Anti-Federalists, 52–53, 55
Articles of Confederation and Perpetual Union
  convention to amend, 27–28, 35, 36–38, 40
  deficiencies of, 26–27, 29–32, **33**
  disputes among states, 35–36
  presidents under, 42
Augustus, 20

Beeman, Richard, 12, 36
Bill of Rights, **63**
  lobbying and, 71
  ratification of, 65
  rights in, 15, 53, 60–62, 64
  Supreme Court and, 78–79, **79**, 80
Blaustein, Albert P., 69
Bonaparte, Napoléon, 67
Boston Tea Party, 17, **18**
Boudinot, Elias, 42
Bouvines, Battle of, 21
Bowdoin, James, 32, 34
Bowen, Catherine Drinker, 46
boycotts, 17
Brown, Henry Billings, 77–78
Brown v. Board of Education (1954), 78
Brownback, Sam, 11
Bryan, Samuel, 28
Buffalo News (newspaper), 80
Burr, Aaron, 61

Bush, George W., 77

Center for Voting and Democracy, 72
chief executives. *See* presidents
Cicero, 19
Citizens United v. Federal Election Commission (2010), 80
Civil War, 75, 76
Code of Hammurabi, 14
Collins, John, 48
colonies, 13, 15, 22–24
commerce, interstate, 35, 46
Congress
  Bill of Rights, 60
  Connecticut Compromise, 44
  current gridlock, 80
  drawing of district boundaries, 72
  people's right to petition, 60
  powers of, 8, 46, 47, 49, 50, 51
  Three-Fifths Compromise, 45–46
  under Virginia Plan, 40–41
Connecticut, 58
Connecticut Compromise, 43–46
Connecticut Resolves, 13
Constitution, **10**
  amendment process, 12, 51
  amendments to, **63**, 65, 76, 78
    See also Bill of Rights
  deficiencies
    drawing of Congressional district boundaries, 72
    influence of political parties, 70–71, 76
    lobbying industry, 71, 73–74
    slavery, 74
  legacy in Europe of, 66–69, **68**
  powers of federal government, 8, 46–47, 49–50
  Preamble to, 51
  ratification of

achievement of, 58, **59**
celebrations for, 58–60
opponents of, 52–53, 55–56, **55**
process for, 51
proponents of, 56–58, 70–71
selection of president, 49, 77
supremacy of federal laws, 52
Constitutional Convention (1787)
adjournment, 51
call for, 27–28, 35, 36–38
delegates, 39–40, **41**
Great Compromise, 43–46
opposition of Rhode Island to, 39–40, 48
original mandate, 40
Three-Fifths Compromise, 45–46
Virginia Plan, 40–42, 47, 49
Continental Congress
under Articles of Confederation, 26–27
first meeting, 17
payment of war debts, 27
Shays's Rebellion and, 33–34
during War of Independence, 18, 29, 30
continentals (money), 29–30, 31, **33**
Cornwallis, Charles, 18, **28**
Cosby, William, 53–54
Court of Star Chamber, 62
Cutler, Manasseh, 32

Dale, Thomas, 23
Dayton, Thomas, 39
Declaration of Independence (1776), 17, 26, 43
Declaration of the Rights of Man and of the Citizen (1789), 66–67
Declaratory Act (1767), 17
De La Warre, Baron, 23
Delaware, 58
Dickinson, John, 43
Dred Scott decision (1857), 75–76

economy, 29–30
Eighth Amendment, 62
Electoral College, 49, 77
Eleventh Amendment, 65
Ellsworth, Oliver, 45

Federalist Papers, 56–58, 70–71

feudal system, 20
Fifth Amendment, 62
Fillmore, Millard, 37
First Amendment, 60, 71, 80
Fourteenth Amendment, 72, 76, 78
Fourth Amendment, 62
France, 30, 66–68, **68**
Franklin, Benjamin, 41
at Constitutional Convention, 39, 43–46
continentals (money) and, 31
on importance of compromising, 44
opposition to slavery, 74
freedom of the press, 53–55, 60
freedom of speech
in Constitution, 53, 60
in Rome, 19
Supreme Court decision about, 80
French and Indian War (1754–1763), 15

Gates, Thomas, 23
gay rights, 78
Georgia, 58
Germany, 68, 69
Gerry, Elbridge, 39, 72
gerrymandering, 72
Gore, Al, 77
Gorham, Nathaniel, 42
Grant, Ulysses S., 73
Great Britain, 15–17, 20–22
Great Compromise, 43–46
Great Depression, 74
Griffin, Cyrus, 42

Hamilton, Alexander
Constitutional Convention
call for, 27–28, 36
as delegate to, 39, 46
death of, 61
on establishing firm foundation for US, 25
Federalist Papers, 56–58
political parties and, 70
as Secretary of Treasury, 61
on Shays's Rebellion, 34
Hamilton, Andrew, 54
Hammurabi, Code of, 14
Hamor, Ralph, 24

Hancock, John
  as president under Articles of
    Confederation, 42
  Shays's Rebellion and, 34, 37
Hanson, John, 42
health care, 8–12
Henry, Patrick, 55–56, **55**
Hitler, Adolf, 69
homes, protection against soldiers in,
  60–61
House of Burgesses, 25
House of Commons (Great Britain), 21

inflation, 29–30
interstate commerce, 35, 46
Intolerable Acts (1774), 17
Isaacson, Walter, 44
Italy, 68, 69

Jackson, Andrew, 76
Jamestown, Virginia, 22–24
Jay, John, 56–57
Jefferson, Thomas, 17, **41**
John (king of England), 21–22, **23**
judicial system
  created by Constitution, 49–50
  created by the Magna Carta, 22
  rights of individuals in, 62
  See also Supreme Court

King, Rufus, 39
Knox, Henry, 34

law of reciprocity, 73
Laws Divine, Moral and Martial (Virginia
  colony), 23–24
Lee, Richard Henry
  opposition to Constitution, 52, 53
  president under Articles of
    Confederation, 42
  on Shays's Rebellion, 34
Levinson, Jessica, 80
libel, 54
lighthorsemen, 32
lobbying industry, 71, 73–74, 79
Louis XVI (king of France), 66, 67, **68**

Madison, James

background of, 19
belief in strong federal government, 27
at Constitutional Convention, 39
  on absence of Rhode Island, 40
  Virginia Plan, 40–42, 47, 49
Federalist Papers, 56–58
on Henry's opposition to ratification, 56
on political parties, 70–71
as president, 61
Magna Carta (1215), 20–22, **23**
Martin, Luther, 45, 46
Maryland, 58
Maryland Act for the Liberties of the
  People, 13
Massachusetts
  ratification by, 58
  Shays's Rebellion, 30–34
  slavery outlawed in, 45
Massachusetts Body of Liberties (1641),
  13
Mayflower Compact, 24
medical care, 8–12
medieval era, 20–22
Mieroop, Marc Van De, 14
Mifflin, Thomas, 39, 42
money, 29–30, 31, 33
Montfort, Earl Simon de, 22
Morris, Gouverneur, 51

Napoleón Bonaparte, 67
Necessary and Proper Clause, 50
New Deal, 74
New Hampshire, 58
New Jersey, 58
New Jersey Plan, 43
New York, 53–55, 56, 58
New York Weekly Journal (newspaper), 54
Ninth Amendment, 64
North Carolina, 59–60

Obama, Barack, 9
Octavius, 20
oligarchy, 52, 67
Otis, James, 16

paper money, 29–30, 31, **33**
Parliament, 21, 22
Paterson, William, 42, 43

Patient Protection and Affordable Care
   Act (2012), 8–12
Pennsylvania, 58, 64
Pennsylvania Gazette (newspaper), 74
Plessy v. Ferguson (1896), 76–78
Plymouth Colony, 24
pocket boroughs, 21
political parties, 70–73, 76, 80
presidents
   under Articles of Confederation, 42
   election of, 49, 77
   judicial system and, 49–50
   under New Jersey Plan, 43
   powers under Constitution, 49–50
   under Virginia Plan, 40, 47, 49
Publius (pseudonym), 56
punishments, protection against cruel, 62

Rakove, Jack N., 52–53
Randolph, Edmund, 40, 42, 50
Reform Act (Great Britain, 1832), 21
Regulators, 31–34
religious freedom, 24, 60
representation and taxation, 16
Revere, Paul, 31
Revolutionary War. *See* War of
   Independence
Rhode Island
   absence from Constitutional
      Convention, 39–40, 48
   ratification and, 58, 59, 60
right to assembly, 53, 60
right to own guns, 60
right to petition government, 60, 71
right to privacy, 78
Roberts, John, 9, 11
Robespierre, Maximilien de, 67
Roe, Mark, 27
Roe v. Wade (1973), 78
Roman Republic, 18–20
Romulus, 19
Russia, 68–69

searches, protection against unreasonable,
   62
Second Amendment, 60, 78–79, 79
Seneca, 19
"separate but equal" standard, 76–78

separation of church and state, 60
Seventh Amendment, 62
Shays, Daniel, 31–34, 37
Shays's Rebellion, 30–34
Sherman, Roger, 43
Shirer, William L., 69
Silver, Nate, 72
Sixth Amendment, 62
slavery/slaves, 47
   abolition of, 45, 74–76
   importation of, 46
   Three-Fifths Compromise, 45–46
social Darwinism, 77–78
soldiers housed in private homes, 15,
   60–61
South Carolina, 58
"spoils" system, 76
St. Clair, Arthur, 42
Stamp Act (1765), 16–17
Stamp Act Congress, 16–17
Star Chamber, 62
states
   under Articles of Confederation, 26–27,
      35–36
   under Constitution
      federal regulation of interstate
         commerce, 46
      protection from lawsuits in federal
         courts, 65
      right to establish militias, 60
      supremacy of federal laws, 52
   debt and, 29–30, 33
   fear of powerful federal government,
      41–43, 55–56
Strauss, David A., 9
Sugar Act (1764), 15–16
Supremacy Clause, 52
Supreme Court
   abolition decision, 75–76
   abortion decision, 78
   Constitutional provisions about, 49–50
   current issues before, 78–79, 79
   freedom of speech of corporations
      decision, 80
   health care decision, 8–9, 11
   separate but equal decisions, 76–78

Tacitus, 19

Taney, Roger B., 76
tariffs/taxes
    under Articles of Confederation,
        29, 30
    under Constitution, 8–9, 46,
        50
    imposed by King John, 21–22
    representation and, 16
    during Revolution, 29
    on whiskey, 64
Tarquinius Superbus, 19
Tea Act (1773), 17
Tenth Amendment, 64
Third Amendment, 60–61
Thirteenth Amendment, 76
Three-Fifths Compromise, 45–46
Thurber, James, 73
Townshend Acts (1767), 17
trade, 35, 46
Treaty of Ghent (1814), 61
trial, individual's rights, 62
trial by jury, 16, 62
Turner, Douglas, 80
Twelve Tables (450 BC), 19, 20

Virginia, 22–24, 58

Virginia Plan, 40–42, 47, 49
voting rights, British women's, 21

War of 1812, 61
War of Independence
    conduct of, 17, 18, 26
    debts from, 27, 29–30, 48, 50
    fake continentals (money), 31
    French aid, 66
    Hamilton during, 61
Washington, George, 41
    belief in strong federal government, 27
    Constitutional Convention and, 39–40,
        43
    Continental Army, 18
    on continentals (money), 31
    on political parties, 70
    Whiskey Rebellion and, 64
West, Thomas, 22–23
Whiskey Rebellion (1794), 64
Wilson, James, 49, 50
women, voting rights in Britain, 21
World War I, 68, 69
World War II, 69

Zenger, John Peter, 54–55

Picture Credits

Cover: Thinkstock Images

© Bettmann/Corbis: 33, 55, 63, 75

© Julie Dermansky/Corbis: 79

© Heritage Images/Corbis: 28

© PoodlesRock/Corbis: 18, 41, 47

Thinkstock Images: 6, 7, 10, 23

Steve Zmina: 59

Execution of Louis XVI (1754–93) 21st January 1793 (coloured engraving) (see also 154902), French School, (18th Century)/ Bibliotheque Nationale, Paris, France/Giraudon/The Bridgeman Art Library: 68

About the Author

Hal Marcovitz is a former newspaper reporter and the author of more than 150 books for young readers. He grew up in Philadelphia and makes his home in Bucks County, Pennsylvania, one of three original counties established by Pennsylvania founder and proprietor William Penn. His other titles in the Understanding American History series include *The 1960s*, *The History of Rock and Roll*, and *The Roaring Twenties*.